Happy Birthday!

W9-BYF-752

Smile, God Loves You a Bunch

QUIET TIMES WITH JESUS

REVIEW AND HERALD® PUBLISHING ASSOCIATION
HAGERSTOWN, MD 21740

Copyright © 1992
Review and Herald® Publishing Association

The authors assume full responsibility for the accuracy of all facts and quotations as cited in this book.

This book was
Edited by Penny Estes Wheeler
Designed by Bill Kirstein
Cover art by Byron Steele
Cover photo by Todd Park
Type set: 11/13 Melior

PRINTED IN U.S.A.

97 96 95 94 93 92   10 9 8 7 6 5 4 3 2

R & H Cataloging Service

Quiet times with Jesus.

   1. Children—Religious life. 2. Devotional
literature—Juvenile. 3. Devotional calendars—
Seventh-day Adventist.

                242.62

ISBN 0-8280-0678-4

Contributing Authors

Mary H. Duplex is the author of three children's books and has had numerous short stories published in *Guide, Primary Treasure*, and *Our Little Friend*. She has four grown children and 15 grandchildren. She lives in Washington State with her husband, Sid, and their miniature schnauzer name Schultzie.

Faith Johnson Crumbly's professional roles have included speechwriter and ghostwriter for business executives, editor and writer for business and community newsletters, and writer for community newspapers. But for many more years her "heart-writing" has produced plays, poetry, songs, speeches, and programs for the children in her home, home churches, and church and public schools. She has been published in magazines, including *Insight, Kids' Stuff, Lake Union Herald*, and *Cornerstone Connections*. Faith says that her favorite audience and the heroes in much of her writing are her husband, Edward, and their five children.

Cheryl Holloway has a B.S. in early childhood and elementary education and an M.A. in education, neither of which was full preparation for her role as mother of four children, ages 4-10. Cheryl has taught church school in Indonesia and home school in Michigan. She and her husband, David, and their children live on the Blackfeet Indian reservation beside Glacier National Park. Currently she is in charge of the Early Childhood Education Department at the Blackfeet Community College. She has written numerous materials for children and young adults, as well as two books, *Time Out for Moms* and *Creative Devotions*.

A former grade school teacher, **Virginia L. Kroll** has been writing for only seven years. But in that short time she has had an incredible 1,600 articles/stories accepted by juvenile magazines, as well as 14 picture books. She is currently a full-time writer-lecturer and mother of six children. She has an 18-month-old granddaughter.

Though a librarian and teacher by profession, **Eileen E.**

Lantry's first love is nature. She enjoys studying nature, collecting from " 'God's second book,' and teaching in all its forms." Her three sons, two grandsons, and her students from kindergarten to college have benefited from this interest.

The Lantrys spent 14 years as missionaries in the Far East, mostly in Singapore and Sabah. Eileen enjoys giving Bible studies, hiking, camping, and cross-country skiing. She has published 13 books and many stories and articles, but she says that the most important thing in her life is that she loves Jesus.

Patty Mostert Marsh of Centralia, Missouri, spends quality time with her husband, Larry, and their two teenage daughters. She also makes time for writing amid her responsibilities as a teacher at Sunnydale Academy and busy vocalist-pianist. Her articles have been published in magazines, including *Celebration* and *Mid-America Adventist Outlook*.

Patty encourages young mothers to "cherish the time you spend with your children. You will never regret it."

Charles Mills writes from his home office near Hagerstown, Maryland. He and his wife, Dorinda, operate Christian Communications, producing media products for a wide variety of clients, including the General Conference of Seventh-day Adventists.

Born to missionary parents, Mills spent many years in the Far and Middle East. A 1973 graduate of Southern Missionary College, Charles has worked as a film/video producer, radio station manager, school teacher, and professional pilot.

"If I have one message for today's Adventist parents," Mills says, "it's this: read to your children. Introduce them to Jesus through the wonderful materials prepared by our Adventist publishing houses."

Nina Coombs Pykare, of Warren, Ohio, has been writing ever since she could hold a pencil, but her first work was published when she was about 9. A long poem about Jesus feeding the 5,000, it appeared in the office paper where her father worked.

Nina loves to write and has had 40 books and almost 300 stories published. She has eight children and five grandchildren and says that God has been very good to her, giving her lots of stories to write and people to love.

Colleen L. Reece lived in the woods of Washington State when she was a child. Her home was so far out of town that the family had no electricity, so Colleen learned to read under the warm yellow glow of a kerosene lamp.

Colleen always wanted to write books, and she accepted the Lord Jesus into her heart when she was just a little girl.

Many years later God answered Colleen's prayers. She has had 57 books published, including *JumpStart*; *Sandwich Island Summer*; *The Mysterious Treadle Machine*; *Plain, Plain Melissa Jane*; and *PK the Great.* She has had articles published in many magazines, including *Vibrant Life*, *Signs of the Times*, *Guide*, and *Our Little Friend.*

Carol Barron Thomas, editorial secretary for *Message* and *Junior Teen Plus*, cherishes memories of growing up in New Jersey with her four brothers and three sisters. "My parents, Edward and Cora Barron, played with us," she says. "Daddy taught me how to skate and play baseball."

Carol, whose husband, Clarence L. Thomas III, is an ordained minister, is the mother of three grown children, Clarence IV, Donna-Maria, and Torrence. The Thomases were missionaries for 12 years in Brazil and the Caribbean, and Carol writes about some of their experiences.

VeraLee Wiggins lives in College Place, Washington, with her husband and her granddaughter, Julie. She has four grown children and seven grandchildren.

VeraLee loves animals almost more than anything, especially the family Pomeranian, Little Lady Nika Fantasia, also known as Bunky. She takes lots of pictures, mostly of Julie and Bunky. She also enjoys music a lot. She and her husband have music in their office all the time they work. In the spring the family eagerly waits for good weather so they can pile into their pickup and fifth-wheel trailer for weekends of fun and relaxation.

Introduction

This preschool devotional book is designed to provide stories and activities for a six-month time period. Children of this age enjoy repetition, and parents and teachers are encouraged to use the book again and again.

It is divided into three sections. The first section, by Cheryl Holloway, consists of 30 family worship activities. Because these are more than stories, most require advance planning. To avoid confusion, adults will want to look over the activity and make certain they are prepared for it before beginning.

Stories in the central portion of the book cover a wide variety of topics. The editors have taken care to include stories about children in many different situations, reflecting various family situations. In many cases authors used the actual names of the children involved. Where the names could seem unusual, we have added a guide to pronunciation.

The last portion of the book (30 readings) is written by Charles Mills and tells the story of Terry's move to the city. It is a continued story, but written so that each devotion stands on its own.

Dedication

Dedicated to the little ones and those who teach them to walk and talk in the light of Jesus' love.

Family Worship
Activities

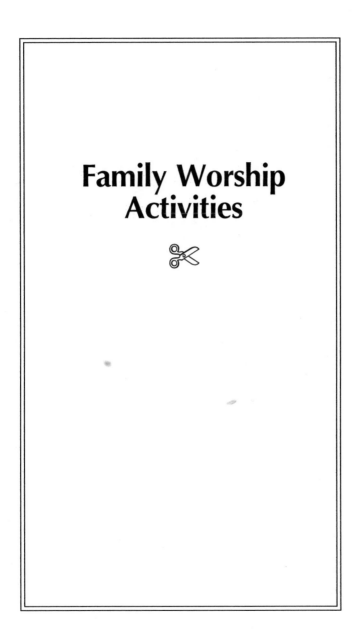

Hide-and-Seek

We're going to play hide-and-seek as part of our devotions tonight! Who wants to be "it" first? *(Let a child hunt first. On the last round of the game, you should be "it." When you have finished counting and you call "Ready or not, here I come," instead of looking for the rest of the family, sit down and read a book or magazine. When the rest of the family finally realizes you aren't coming to find them and they come out of hiding, give them the following explanation.)*

How did you feel when I didn't even try to find you? Did you feel left out and lonely? Sometimes God feels lonely too. Did you know that? In our verse for today, God says, "I was ready to be found, but no one looked for me. . . . I said 'Here I am! Here I am!' to people who didn't want Me" (Isaiah 65:1, paraphrase).

God is saying "Here I am! Here I am!" to us, right now! We should tell Him, "We see You, God! We want You to be our friend, and be part of our family! We want You to know we love You! And we don't ever want You to feel lonely, because we want You to be close to us."

Let's pray, and tell that to God now, shall we? And then we'll play another game of hide-and-seek, and I'll play right this time!—C.H.

A Garland and a Chain of Honor

Needed: real or silk leaves or flowers woven or tied into a garland, and/or a ribbon attached to a paper or metal medallion.

Do you remember seeing pictures of Olympic winners? When these people win races or jumping or diving contests, the people in charge of the Olympics put ribbons and metals around their necks. Then everyone claps and cheers "Hurray"! That's the way we tell the winners how proud we are of them. They've worked hard to become the best, and we honor them.

Did you know that the Bible says that obeying Dad and Mom is very important too? King Solomon wrote in Proverbs, "Attend, my son, to your father's instruction and do not reject your mother's teaching; they become you like a garland on your head, a chain of honour for your neck" (Prov. 1:8, 9, REB).

All the important things Mom and Dad teach you are like this lovely garland on your head, and this beautiful medal of honor around your neck. When people see you doing the things you should, they will honor you! They will say, "Hurray for _____ (your child's name)! They will be proud of you, because they can see you are wise.

God gave you a mother and father in order to help you. We can help you grow up to be happy. We can show you how to work. We can teach you about what is good and bad. We can help you learn good ways to treat people. And what you learn will be like this beautiful garland and medal of honor. It will make you look great!

(Note to Readers: If you choose, take part of your family devotion time during the next few weeks to discuss wise choices you notice your child making during the day. As often as possible, let him or her wear the garland and/or chain during devotions as a recognition of how he or she is learning to follow good advice.)—C.H.

A Light

Needed: a darkened room and a flashlight. Place stools and other obstacles on the floor between the door and your Bible, which you've placed somewhere on the other side of the room. Tape the wall light switch shut.

Tell your child, "My Bible is in the _____ on the _____ . Can you go get it for me? It will be dark in there, but don't turn on the light."

When your child comes back with the Bible, talk about his/her experiences in the dark room. Ask, "Did you have a hard time finding the Bible? Did you stumble over anything? What did you need to help you in that dark room?"

Proverbs 6:23 says that "these commands are a lamp, this teaching is a light" (NIV). The things Mom and Dad teach you from the Bible help you like a light in a dark room! The things God says show you where problems are, and they tell you what to do so you won't run into trouble and get hurt! What God says helps you decide the best way to go, so you will be happy.

Let's think of some things Mom and Dad and God ask you to do. One thing we say is "Always tell the truth." How is the commandment "Thou shalt not bear false witness" like a light? Does it show you a big problem you could bump into if you didn't tell the truth? Lying makes trouble, doesn't it? If you tell a lie, Mom and Dad can't believe what you say anymore. You might be telling the truth, but no one can know for sure. You could even be punished for something you didn't do, because your parents couldn't believe you when you told the truth.

Lying always makes trouble. But if you obey the commandment "Don't lie," you won't ever get into trouble because of a lie you told.

Let's go into that dark room again, and see what help a flashlight can be!

(Note to Readers: Just for fun, you might want to have a small treat hidden in the room that your child can find by using the flashlight.)—C.H.

Bouncing Light

Needed: mirror, flashlight, matte black paper or easily obtainable object.

Shine the flashlight into the mirror and watch the wall or floor for the light that bounces off the mirror. By moving the mirror, you can make the spot of light dance around the room.

The Bible says, "The Lord is God, and he has made his light shine upon us" (Ps. 118:27, NIV). God is like the flashlight, and He is shining on us. We can be like the mirror, and share His love and goodness and light all around us! Or we could be like this black paper. What happens when the light shines on this? Does it go anywhere else? No, we see a bright spot on the paper, but hardly any of the light bounces anywhere else.

When the light bounces off the mirror, we call it a reflection. I'm going to do something that will reflect, too. *(Smile warmly at your child. Smile at other family members too, until everyone is smiling back at you.)* See all the happy faces that reflect my smile?

Smiling makes us feel warm and good inside. So when we smile at others, we are not only passing on a happy face; we are passing on warm feelings, and helping other people feel better! Can you think of other things we can do that share the light that God is giving us?

(Note to Readers: Discuss your child's ideas, and help him or her decide on something special to do in the near future.)—C.H.

Shadow Fun

Needed: white typing paper (or other thin paper) glued to cardboard frame, small objects like scissors, eating and cooking utensils, pen or pencil, large safety pin, screw, nail, washers, curlers, stapler, watch, etc.

Hold the paper and cardboard shadow theater near a light source such as a window or lamp. Hold each object behind the paper screen so it makes a shadow for your child to identify. Older children might be more challenged if you hold the objects a small distance away from the screen so the image is blurred. Try holding two objects together so the images mix, and ask if your child can identify both objects.

Can you tell me what a shadow is? Is it hard or soft? You can't feel a shadow, can you? A shadow is made when the light doesn't hit the paper, because it is stopped by something. *(Hold up several objects and let the child tell you what is stopping the light. If you have a chance, and the sun is shining brightly, go outside for more discussion.)*

Do you see any shadows out here? Are you making a shadow? What about the house, trees, bushes? How do they make shadows?

On a hot day we like to sit in the shadow of the house or a tree. We call it shade. It feels nice and cool, compared to the hot sun. Maybe David was enjoying the cool shade of a rock when He wrote the verse we have for today. "He who dwells in the shelter of the Most High will rest in the shadow of the Almighty" (Ps. 91:1, NIV).

David knew He was safe in God's shadow. Of course, God's shadow didn't protect David from the sun, like the shadow from a rock. But it protected him from many things that could have hurt him. Can you think of some?

We can't touch God's shadow. We can't see God's shadow, like we can see other shadows. But sometimes we can feel when God is close to us. He often helps us feel calm and unafraid in a scary time. But even when we don't feel God, we know He's there, because He promised to watch over us and take care of us, and we can see many of the things He does for us.

Can you name some of the nice things God has done for you?—C.H.

Symmetry

Needed: several pairs of scissors, paper (can be colored), pair of mittens and/or shoes, yardstick (optional).

Fold small pieces of paper in half and cut out shapes on the fold, so when the papers are opened, the whole figure can be seen. Hearts, Christmas trees, and paper dolls are some examples. Use your imagination and cut out some unique shapes, and let your child cut out figures, too.

We call a shape symmetrical when it is the same on both sides of its middle line. The folded line is the middle of our paper cutouts, and the shapes are the same on both sides of the line. Look around the room and see whether you can find any other things that have symmetry.

Is your chair symmetrical? What about the lamp? Can you find a middle line on your windows? You might be able to find several middle lines on some objects. You can use a yardstick to help you imagine a middle line. What about your house? your car? your bed? your cat, dog, or bird?

Look at yourself. Where is your middle line? Of course, we can't fold you, but put your arms out and match up your thumb and fingers. They match almost like you had been cut out. Are they the same? Try putting the same mitten on both hands. It will fit on one hand, but not on the other. Your hands look like they are the same, but they aren't really the same. They are mirror images of each other.

Many things God made are symmetrical. When you take a walk, look for symmetrical things. Look at the flowers, mushrooms, leaves, seed pods, and seeds. How carefully God made these beautiful things. He is a God of order, and even His designs follow certain patterns of order.

The Bible says, "God is not one who likes things to be disorderly and upset. He likes harmony" (1 Cor. 14:33, TLB). We can see that is true wherever we look!—C.H.

Broken Walls

Needed: a sandpile (such as the beach!) or blocks.

Let's build a house, because we are going to be talking about walls for our devotions. *(Let your child stack blocks to make a simple house.)*

Why do you think walls are such an important part of buildings? What do you think would happen if the walls of our house fell down when it began to storm? Anything could come into our house and wreck it. The wind could blow all our things away, the rain would ruin what was left, and we would be cold and scared!

Break down one of the walls in the building you made, and let's talk about it a little while before we fix it.

No one wants to live in a house or city whose walls are broken down. But some of us do. Do you know who? The Bible says that people who can't control themselves are "like a city whose walls are broken down" (Prov. 25:28, NIV).

We lose control over ourselves when we have bad feelings that make us do wrong things. Sometimes we yell, or throw things, or stomp our feet. We may say things that hurt others. We have let our walls of self-control fall down, and Satan can get in and make trouble. Satan uses these times to wreck the love that holds our family close together.

When we get angry or frustrated or have other feelings that we can't control, we need to ask God to help us. He will help us take care of our bad feelings before they make us do what is wrong. He can even take bad feelings away, and give us the right kind of feelings. It's important to have strong, solid walls on our house. But it's even more important to keep control of ourselves, so Satan can't use us to hurt people.

Why don't you fix the walls of the house you built? Then we'll pray that God will help us keep the walls of our hearts strong!—C.H.

Good News

Needed: a hot day, a pitcher of cold water, water glasses, letter-writing materials.

Let your child pour water for everyone, and enjoy it together. Then read Proverbs 25:25: "Like cold water to a weary soul is good news from a distant land" (NIV).

Water tastes especially good when we are tired and hot. It helps us feel refreshed and rested. Can you remember a time when you were really thirsty, and you couldn't wait to get a drink? All you could think was *Water! Water! Where is some water? (Discuss your child's experiences with being thirsty.)*

People who have loved ones far away get lonely. Hearing good news about their family and friends makes them feel as good as a drink of water makes you feel when you are thirsty.

Do you have a grandma or grandpa who lives far away? What about other family members or friends who might be lonely for some news from you? Let's choose someone to write to. We'll write a family letter full of good news that will make him or her feel special and loved.—C.H.

Secret in a Seed

Needed: a variety of raw seeds that split easily, such as peanut, avocado, peach, bean (Some seeds may need to soak before they can be split.); other seeds, perhaps collected on walks.

Did you know that seeds have coats? They wear them to protect their special secrets inside. Some seeds, like peach pits, have very tough coats. Others split off easily when the seed has swelled with water. Let's take off the seed coat on our seed.

Do you see a place where we can split open this seed? When we open the seed, we can see the special secret in it. It's a tiny new plant! Every seed has a baby plant inside of it, ready and waiting to grow.

In every seed, no matter how tiny, God puts a little piece of life. Then He helps that little piece of life grow up into a wonderful part of His world! Jesus told a story about a tiny mustard seed.

"Jesus asked, 'What is the kingdom of God like? What shall I compare it to? It is like a mustard seed, which a man took and planted in his garden. It grew and became a tree, and the birds of the air perched in its branches' " (Luke 13:18, 19, NIV).

God made little pictures of the way His kingdom works in the billions of seeds all over the world! He says to us, "See how easy it is to love Me, and be a part of My kingdom? You are like the little seed. I put a little bit of life in you. That was My present to you. Now all you need to do is let Me help you grow!"—C.H.

Growing Like a Seed

Needed: bean seeds soaked overnight, paper towels, saucer, dark spot (or cover for saucer).

Our seeds look dead, all wrapped up in their dry little coats. But they don't need very much to start growing. They just need water and a warm dark place to grow.

Let's put our bean seeds between several layers of paper towels and lay them on the saucer. You can dampen them. They need to stay wet, but they will die if they lie in water for a long time. Now let's put them in a warm, dark place. We will check on them every day to make sure they are wet enough and see how they are growing.

Let's put the flower seeds in the pot and water them, too. We won't be able to see the flower seeds sprout, but we will be able to see the little plant come up, when it reaches for the sun.

Jesus told a story about a farmer who went out to sow his seed. Some of his seed fell on the hard path, and birds ate it up. Some of the seed fell on rocky ground, where there was hardly any soil to hold food or water. The seed sprouted, but under the hot sun it dried out and died.

But "still other seed fell on good soil" (Matt. 13:8, NIV). That seed landed in soft soil, where there were warm, dark, damp places to grow. It grew and grew, and produced a fine crop.

Then Jesus said that He is like the farmer. He puts seeds in our hearts. If we take good care of His seeds, they will grow strong, and we will become like beautiful, growing plants in His kingdom. But we have to make sure there is a good place for Jesus' seeds to grow.

The seeds Jesus gives us are the things He tells us in the Bible. We need to listen carefully, and think about what Jesus says many times during the day. And we need to obey Him. Then the seeds He has put in our hearts will grow strong!

Can you name some of the "seeds" Jesus puts in our hearts?

(Note to Readers: kindness, joy, helpfulness. . . .)—C.H.

Reaching to God

Needed: house plant beside a window.

Do you see how the leaves on our plant are aimed toward the window? Why do you think they are doing that? Let's move the plant to the other side of the window. See, the leaves are pointing the wrong way now. The sun won't shine on them. Let's check on our plant for several days, and see if the leaves turn toward the window again.

Plants need the sun to grow. The leaves use the sun to help them make food for the rest of the plant. Do we need sun? We sure do! We get sun when we go outside. Our body needs it to help it make the vitamins we need to grow. We can't make food like plants do, but the sun helps us use the food we eat.

It's a good thing the plants can use the sun to help them make food, because most of the food we eat comes from plants! We wouldn't have any food if the plants didn't make it! Can you think of some foods you eat that come from plants?

The Bible says that we need another kind of sunshine too. In Psalms we read, "Restore us, O God Almighty; make your face shine upon us, that we may be saved" (Ps. 80:7, NIV). Can you imagine God's face shining on us? He must have a big smile on His face. When I think of God's big, smiling, shining face looking at me, I feel warm and good all over, don't you?

It makes me want to be like the leaves of our plant, turning to God all the time, so that I don't miss any of His sunshine! That's why we often sing songs and talk about how good God is. It helps us feel God's shining face! *(Think of a song to sing that will help you feel close to God today.)*—C.H.

Working Together

Needed: hand-operated eggbeater (or other gear-operated machine with observable gears), piece of tape.

Machines help us do work. Our eggbeater is a little machine that helps us mix up our food in the kitchen. Can you see these little teeth on this big wheel? They catch the teeth on the little wheel. Move the handle, and watch the big wheel make the little wheels turn. When the little wheels turn, they turn the beaters that do our work for us!

Let's put a piece of tape on one of the beaters, and count how many times the beaters turn during one turn of the big wheel. Those beaters do a lot of work when we only make one turn. How fast can you make them go?

God made everything in our world work together like these gears on our eggbeaters. The earth moving around the big, warm sun is like a big gear, making the seasons of fall, winter, spring, and summer. The seasons bring the plants to life, help them grow, and put them to sleep. The animals, and we, depend on the plants for food.

Do you see how the sun, the earth, the weather, the plants, and we all move together like gears? And if our world is like the gears on this eggbeater, who do you think turns the handle and gives us energy? I think it must be God! Listen as David describes our world in a psalm.

"The moon marks off the seasons, and the sun knows
    when to go down.

You bring darkness, it becomes night, and all the beasts of the forest prowl.

The lions roar for their prey and seek their food from God.

The sun rises, and they steal away; they return and lie down in their dens.

Then man goes out to his work, to his labor until evening" (Ps. 104:19-23, NIV).

When all of God's world works together, we have peace and happiness.—C.H.

Friction

Needed: crayons, sandpaper, wax paper, regular paper.

What happens when you color on the sandpaper? The rough pieces of sand grab chunks of colored wax. *(If you have several grades of sandpaper, let your child experiment with each grade.)*

What happens when you color on wax paper? The crayon just slides along, doesn't it? It's hard to color on wax paper. Why? There isn't anything rough enough to catch any of the crayon, so nothing comes off and sticks on the wax paper. The wax paper is too much like the wax crayon.

Try coloring on a regular piece of paper. The paper doesn't feel rough to our fingers, but it's just rough enough to catch bits of crayon that leave a mark on the paper. Friction is when something rubs against something else. There was lots of friction between the crayon and the sand paper, and very little between the crayon and the wax paper. The friction was just right for coloring when you drew on the regular paper.

Try using sandpaper to sharpen your crayon tip into a point. Friction is useful! It helped you color, and it sharpened your crayon. You might have seen your dad or mom use a whetstone or a file to sharpen a knife. Solomon says that "as iron sharpens iron, so one man sharpens another" (Prov. 27:17, NIV).

When people live together, their different ideas and ways of doing things rub together. Often there is friction, but it can be good. Someone else's ideas can change your ideas, and help you think in a new and better way. And you can help them have new ideas.

You can remember this when you notice that other people are different from you. You can use this friction to help each other!

How are you different from other people like Grandma and Grandpa? How are you different from some of your friends?—C.H.

Heating Up

Sometimes when my hands get cold, I rub them together. Try it, and see if you can get your hands warm that way. Try rubbing them against your pant legs. We are using friction to warm our hands. Friction happens when two things rub together, and it produces heat.

Sometimes friction makes things get too hot. When someone puts on the car brakes hard and fast, the tires screech as they rub against the pavement, trying to stop. Often you can see a black mark on the road where the tires got hot and left some of their rubber on the road.

When people live together, their different ways of doing things sometimes create friction and trouble. This often happens in families. Jacob and Esau were brothers who were very different. The Bible says, "The boys grew up, and Esau became a skillful hunter, a man of the open country, while Jacob was a quiet man, staying among the tents" (Gen. 25:27, NIV).

These boys didn't like the same kinds of things, and they didn't understand each other. Jacob did something very wrong to Esau. Esau got so angry that Jacob had to run away from home, and he stayed away for a long, long time.

When he finally came back, he was still scared that Esau would be angry with him. But He prayed that God would help him make friends with Esau. He sent lots of presents ahead to Esau, and when Esau came, Jacob bowed seven times, to show Esau that he honored and respected him. Esau hugged him and kissed him, and they were friends again.

This is a good story to remember when things heat up between you and your brothers or sisters or friends. Too much heat can make so much anger and trouble that you won't have friends. But if you respect others who are different from you, and ask God to help you treat them right, you and your family and friends can have good times together. —C.H.

Living Water

Needed: pieces of bread, soft and dried; leaves and/or flowers, fresh and dried.

Jesus said something wonderful to a woman who had come to draw water from a well. He said He could give her living water. He explained that whoever drank the water from the well would get thirsty again, but "whoever drinks the water I give him will never thirst. Indeed, the water I give him will become in him a spring of water welling up to eternal life" (John 4:14, NIV).

Even ordinary water is very special! Every living thing needs it. Did you know that you are made out of mostly water? You don't look wet, because your skin is a special covering that keeps you from drying out. But every cell of your body has water in it.

Feel this bread. It feels soft because it has water in it. When we leave bread out, the water in the bread disappears into the air, and then we have a dry, hard piece of bread, like this. Feel this leaf. It still has lots of water in its cells. This one fell off a tree a long time ago and dried up. See how easily it breaks up? If you rub it between your hands, you can break it into dusty little crumbs.

If all the water in our bodies dried up, we would just be dry dust too. We drink several glasses of water a day, to help our bodies stay healthy and strong.

Jesus knew how much our bodies need water to live. That's why He made rivers, lakes, oceans, clouds, and rain. But He also knew that our hearts need His living water to be happy and healthy. His living water brings love, kindness, and happiness into our lives. When we listen to Him we are drinking His living water, and it will bring us eternal life.— C.H.

Case of the Disappearing Water

Needed: chalkboard or construction paper, hair blow-dryer or paper fan.

Let your child write on the chalkboard or paper with a wet finger. Then give him a blow-dryer or fan, and let him dry up his wet marks with the warm air.

What happened to the watermarks? Where do you think the water is now? The water evaporated into the air. All the water that made the watermarks is in little tiny droplets floating in the air.

The droplets are so tiny we can't see them. We can't see the air, either! We couldn't see the air come out of the blow-dryer, but we did see the work it did. It dried up the water marks.

When the wind blows, we can't see it, but we know it is there because of what it does to the trees and grass. We can feel how hard it pushes against us. Jesus said, "The wind blows wherever it pleases. You hear its sound, but you cannot tell where it comes from or where it is going. So it is with everyone born of the Spirit" (John 3:8, NIV).

Many of the things God does are like the wind. When God changes our hearts into something good and beautiful, we can't see Him do it. But we know He has done it, because we are different. When we ask Him to change our bad feelings into good feelings, we can't see how He does it. But instead of hard, angry feelings, we have softer, more understanding and forgiving feelings.

God is full of surprises! That is one of the things that makes Him so special!—C.H.

The Missing Puzzle Piece

Needed: a simple puzzle (or cut a picture into large puzzle pieces). Pass out all the pieces to members of the family except one of the more important pieces (a face, for instance). Hide this one near the sofa.

Let's all work together and put this puzzle together. Oh, dear! It looks like there's a piece missing. What a hole it makes in our puzzle.

Let's pretend that the missing puzzle piece is hiding someplace because it feels like it's so small and nobody needs it. Maybe it thinks that since all the other pieces are working, it doesn't need to help!

Have you ever felt like you didn't need to help clean up the living room or clear the table? When others are working, you might think nobody will miss you. But each one of the things you do to help our family is important, isn't it?

In Gal. 6:4 Paul says, "Let everyone be sure that he is doing his very best" (TLB). If everyone in our family does his or her very best, and we all work together, we can do some great things! We each have a special place in our family.

Who wants to find the missing piece we need to finish our puzzle? I hid it somewhere near the sofa!—C.H.

Cold and Hot

Needed: hot water in a bowl, and very cold water in another bowl.

Put both hands in the water, one hand in each bowl, for about a minute. Now take them out and tell us how they feel!

One of your hands looks pretty rosy. Does it feel warm? Since your hand was colder than the hot water, the heat in the water went into your hand and made it warmer. It feels good to be warm, doesn't it!

Your other hand was warmer than the cold water, so the heat from your hand went into the cold water, and now your hand feels cold. Rub your hands together to help warm it up.

Looking at TV and videos is a little bit like putting your hands into the bowls of water. Good programs make you feel happy and contented and warm inside! They add good ideas to your mind, like the hot water added heat to your hand.

Bad TV programs take away your good, happy feelings, like the cold water took heat away from your hands. Bad ideas make you feel dirty, unhappy, and empty. It's very important to think about the things we watch, because they change the way we think and feel about ourselves and about other people.

Have you ever watched something that made you feel bad inside? What kinds of things are good for you to see?

Long ago Paul gave us some very good advice in the Bible. He said, "Finally, brothers, whatever is true, whatever is noble, whatever is right, whatever is pure, whatever is lovely, whatever is admirable—if anything is excellent or praiseworthy—think about such things" (Phil. 4:8, NIV). Let's try to look at and think about just good things today.—C.H.

More Than One Way

Needed: paper, scissors, knife, water.

Let's say we need to take a piece of paper off this big sheet of paper. How could we do it? *(Follow the children's suggestions until they run out of ideas, then give them hints for other ideas.)*

We could cut it with the scissors. *(Cut off a piece.)* We could tear off a piece. *(Tear off a piece.)* We could use a knife, too, couldn't we! *(Cut off paper on cutting board. Mention safety.)* Could we burn off a piece? *(Try this if you feel you can do it safely.)*

What else could we do? What happens if we dampen the paper? It pulls apart easily when it's wet, doesn't it! *(Keep experimenting if the children's interest is holding.)*

Look at all the different pieces of paper we have now! Why do you think each one looks different?

In 1 Corinthians 12:6 Paul says that "there are different kinds of working, but the same God works all of them in all men" (NIV). Each one of us can love and help others, but did you know that we each have a different way to do it? Just like there are different ways of getting pieces off this paper.

Some people help others by being their friend. Some people are good at being a boss. Some people like to make things beautiful for others by making music or painting pictures. Some people like to tell stories. Others help by cooking, or cleaning, or making clothes.

What do you like to do to help other people? What you do will be different from what anyone else can do, because God made you special and different. And doing the work God made you to do will make you very happy! —C.H.

Staying Dry Under Water

Needed: paper towel, drinking glass, bucket of water.

Did you know that I can put this paper towel in this bucket of water, and it won't get wet? I'll stuff it in the bottom of this glass, turn the glass upside down, and put the glass all the way under the water. *(Keep the glass straight and upside down.)* Now I'll take the glass out. Is the paper towel wet? No! It's perfectly dry, isn't it?

Now, what if I put the glass with the paper towel inside back in the water, and tilt the glass a little bit. Do you see the air bubbles coming up out of the glass?

When I let the air out, what do you think went inside the glass where the air used to be? Do you think the paper is wet? Let's see. Yes, it sure is. The air inside the glass kept the water from coming in and getting the paper wet. But when we let the air out, the water went in.

You know, we are living in a very dirty, wicked world. It isn't easy to stay clean and pure the way God wants us to be, in such a bad place. But God has a good plan to help us keep our minds thinking good thoughts.

Psalms 119:11 says, "I have hidden your word in my heart that I might not sin against you" (NIV). Thinking about God's words, memorizing them, and singing them keeps bad thoughts out, like the air in the glass keeps the water out!

What special words from God do you want to keep remembering today while you play? They will keep you close to God.—C.H.

Together in Love

Needed: scrap of loosely woven cloth, magnifying glass (optional).

Cut two three-inch squares of material. Show your child how to pull the threads off the sides of one square.

What do you think this cloth is made of? When we look at it closely, we see lots of little threads going this way and that. *(Look at the edge of the material with a magnifying glass, if possible.)*

After we pull it apart, all we have left is a little ball of thread that isn't worth very much. Now pull just one thread out of the pile. It looks pretty thin and weak, doesn't it? But when these thin little threads are all woven together into a cloth, they are useful and strong.

What do we use cloth for? *(With your child, look around the room and see the many ways you use cloth every day.)* We even use scraps for dusting and cleaning up, don't we!

Jesus wants us to work closely together like all the threads in a piece of cloth. He wants all His friends to be like a body that is "joined and held together" so that it "builds itself up in love, as each part does its work" (Eph. 4:16, NIV).

Each one of us is pretty little by ourselves. Mommy and Daddy seem big. But we need other people just like children do. And when all of us come close together in love, Jesus can use us to do important things!—C.H.

Weaving

Needed: Paper in several colors.

Cut the colored paper into one-inch strips. Use a third piece of paper for a base. Tape seven or eight strips of paper down along one edge of the base paper.

Show your child how to weave the loose strips of paper in and out of the strips attached to the base. Perhaps you can name the strips as you weave each one. The first one can be Grandpa, the next one Grandma, and so on, until each member of the family has a strip woven into the paper mat. Use stickers to identify each person's strip, or write the names on them.

The pieces of paper woven together make a special pattern. If one of them is missing, we have a big hole, and our pattern doesn't look nice anymore. Remember when we tried to put our puzzle together, but a piece was missing? The missing piece messed up our puzzle, didn't it?

When God made our world, He made lots of patterns. *(Talk about some.)* Our seasons go round and round in a pattern. We have spring, then summer, then what? Fall! And after fall comes winter, and then spring again! The seasons make a pattern, don't they?

What if one of our seasons quit coming when it was supposed to? What would we miss if summer didn't show up? The fruit trees and garden wouldn't have enough time to grow the food we need before cold weather killed the plants. What would happen if we went right from summer into winter, without fall? The Bible says, "There is a time for everything, and a season for every activity under heaven" Eccl. 3:1, NIV).

God has made a time and a place for everything, and for every person. You are part of the pattern God has made in our world! We all need you!—C.H.

Tricky Stuff

Needed: white sugar and salt in small unmarked containers, magnifying glass.

What do you think I have in these little cups? Can you tell by looking at what's inside? Let's look at the crystals with our magnifying glass. *(Lay a few grains of each kind of crystal out on a smooth surface and see if your child can see a difference.)*

What if you tasted each kind of crystal? Will that help you tell the difference? *(Let your child taste the contents of the two jars.)*

It's pretty easy to tell what's in the cups when we taste the crystals, isn't it! *(Stress that it was safe to taste these things because you knew what they were, even though your child didn't, and he or she could trust you. Stress that a person must never taste something if he or she isn't sure it's safe.)* When you tasted the crystals, you knew for sure what they were. The taste was on *your* tongue, not someone else's. It was *your* experience.

The Bible says, "Taste and see that the Lord is good" (Ps. 34:8, NIV). Of course, we don't taste God like He is salt or sugar! But God is saying, "Hey, check Me out. See what I really am. Don't just listen to what other people think about Me. *Experience* me! Then you will know for yourself whether I am good or not!"

Look around you. Can you see things God has done that are good? When you pray, tell Him that you want to taste Him, and see His goodness. Then keep looking and listening for what He wants to show you!—C.H.

Splatter Fun

Needed: toothbrush, comb or screen, tempera paint (poster paint) or food coloring, paper.

Show your child how to fold a piece of paper in half and cut out a pair of wings, or a bird with its wings spread out. (Look at a picture of a bird, if you like, to help you.) Finger-press the bird so that it lies flat on a piece of paper. Help your child dip the toothbrush into a little bit of paint, and brush it across the comb or piece of screen, making splatters on the bird and paper. Your child may want to practice making splatters on another piece of paper until he or she understands how.

Lots of things in this old world can mess us up and make us feel bad and dirty. But we have a special kind of umbrella that can keep us clean! *(Lift up the bird, and look at the clean, white shape underneath.)*

Jesus wants to cover us, like a mother bird covers her chicks to keep them safe. With Jesus' wings over us, we can stay as clean and pure and happy as this clean paper under the bird.

When we think about Jesus, we don't need to worry, even though bad things happen. We know He is always with us. He helps us know how to feel, and He helps us know what to do. We just need to pray the prayer David prayed when he was in trouble: "Hide me in the shadow of your wings" (Ps. 17:8, NIV).

(Either you or your child can write this verse at the bottom of the splatter picture, and hang it up where you both can see it often!)—C.H.

Inside, Outside

Needed: a smooth, rock (one that has been worn smooth by the elements is best), rag, hammer.

Let your child wrap the rock in the rag, and show him or her how to break it with a hammer. Open the rag and examine the pieces of rock. Try putting the pieces together like a puzzle.

Can you tell which sides of the broken pieces used to be the outside of the rock? Describe what the outside of the rock looks and feels like. What does the inside of the rock look like? It's quite different, isn't it!

Many rocks look plain and ordinary on the outside. Being out in the weather changes them. Some stones are washed down rivers. They bang against other rocks and rub against the sand and dirt, and they become smooth on the outside. But they are full of surprises on the inside! When we crack them open, we can see what the real stone is like.

People are like this too! You can't always tell what someone is like on the inside by just looking at the outside. Some people are very beautiful on the outside, but they don't have very good hearts. Other people look plain and ordinary, like a rock, but they are full of wonderful surprises. They may be full of interesting stories or jokes. They may have special hobbies, like collecting stamps or train engine models that they can tell you about. It's fun to find out interesting things about the people we meet.

Remember when Samuel was trying to pick a king from one of Jessie's sons? God told him, "The Lord does not look at the things man looks at. Man looks at the outward appearance, but the Lord looks at the heart" (1 Sam. 16:7, NIV).

God looks on the inside of us, and this is what He loves! We too can learn to love people for who they are rather than what they look like.

Why don't you look around your neighborhood for someone you don't know very well. Perhaps you can invite that person home for supper, and find out something special about him or her!—C.H.

Molded Like Clay

Needed: oil-based clay, bowl of water.

Help your child roll the clay into a ball, and try to float it in the bowl of water. What happens? Ask your child if he or she knows of some way to make the clay float, and let him or her experiment.

It seems impossible for this heavy lump of clay to float, doesn't it? But it can. But try molding it into a cup shape. Now put it carefully in the water. It floats! We didn't take any clay away. We didn't make it lighter. We just changed its shape!

When a potter works with clay he or she changes the shape of the clay into something useful, like a bowl or a pot. In the Bible Isaiah says, "Lord, you are our Father. We are the clay, you the potter; we are all the work of your hand" (Isa. 64:8, NIV).

We are like balls of clay that sink. Even though we want to be good, we can't. Even though we don't want to, we get mad, or disobey, or say things we shouldn't. But when God changes the inside of us, it is easy for us to do good. It is as easy as floating a cup-shaped piece of clay!

We don't have to work hard at being good—it's God that does the work. God changes our hearts so that it is easy for us to do good. But we do have to let Him change us! When we put ourselves in His hands and ask Him to be our Potter, He can make us into something beautiful that He can use. —C.H.

Stories

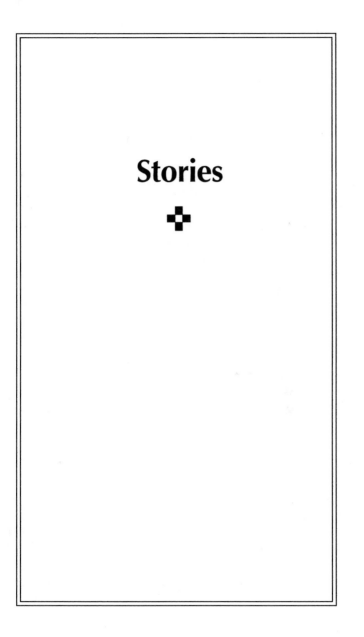

A Monster Did It

Save me, O Lord, . . . from deceitful tongues. Ps. 120:2, NIV.

Shane turned away from the window. It was no fun to visit Grandma when it rained. He couldn't play in the field or go down by the creek.

Shane took his new super bounce ball out of his pocket. Mom had said not to bounce it in the house. But she didn't say he couldn't play with it. Shane tossed the ball high in the air. It hit the ceiling and came down hard. He tried to catch it. The ball bounced off the edge of the end table. Shane lunged for it, but the ball shot past him. Shane fell against the table, and the lamp crashed to the floor.

"Uh-oh," Shane gasped. "Now I'm in trouble."

"What was that noise?" Grandma called. Shane had just enough time to snatch up the ball before she came into the room.

When she saw the broken lamp, Grandma said, "How did that happen?"

"A monster did it," Shane said, hiding the ball behind his back.

"A monster?" Grandma looked around. "I don't see any muddy footprints. Where did the monster go? How did it get out?"

"Well, it turned into a big green bird," Shane said in a rush. "It knocked over the lamp and flew up the fireplace chimney."

"How terrible," said Grandma. "I've never seen any monsters or big green birds around here."

Shane looked down at his toes. "It wasn't a monster or a bird. It was me." He brought the ball out from behind him. "I was playing with this and I broke the lamp. I'm sorry, Grandma."

"I'm glad it wasn't a monster or a bird," said Grandma. "I'm glad it was a boy who isn't afraid to tell the truth." She gave Shane a hug. "Now go get the broom and the dustpan."—M.H.D.

Seeds of Joy

Your joy may be full. John 16:24, KJV.

Xandi (ZAN-dee) raced toward the door of her house, with Beverly close behind her. "You're ugly!" Beverly shouted as Xandi flew through the door.

Xandi brushed a tear off her nose as she walked down the hall to the bathroom. "I'm not ugly," she mumbled as she looked at herself in the mirror on the wall. But she didn't look like the girl who'd rushed outside to play that morning. That happy Xandi had worn a smile that showed a dimple in her right cheek. The sad Xandi in the mirror had her lips poked out, and when she pulled them in, they drooped on each side.

"I just can't keep my lips turned up at the corners when I play with Beverly," Xandi said to herself. She pushed the corners of her lips upward with her fingers. But they slid right back down.

"Smiles start on the inside, sweetheart." Xandi turned around and saw her mother standing in the doorway. "Jesus plants a little seed of joy inside our hearts," Mama said. "When we have joy on the inside, we say kind words. We can even smile at people who are mean to us."

Xandi squeezed her mother's outstretched hand. "Let's help the joy seed grow," she said. "I'm going to pray for it right now."

So Xandi and Mama held hands and bowed their heads. "Dear Jesus," Xandi prayed, "I want Your joy seed to grow in my heart—real big, so big that even Beverly can see my joy. Thank You for helping me."

"Amen," Mama said. "Now let's see your lips turn up! What a beautiful smile you have, Xandi!"—F.J.C.

A Plan to Grow On

Those who work to bring peace are happy. Matt. 5:9, ICB.

"Today I won't come running home crying, Mama!" Xandi said. "I'm going to be like Jesus, just like we talked about in worship this morning."

"But you're wearing your flowered sneakers, Xandi," Mama said. "You know Beverly always makes fun of them."

"I'll say, 'These are my Beverly Laughing Sneakers. I'm glad you enjoy them!' Then I'll laugh too."

"But what if Beverly bangs her Big Wheel into the back of your tricycle again, Xandi?"

"I'll say, 'I'll ride over on the grass so you can get by, Beverly. I'll follow you for a while.' "

"But what if Beverly throws Buffy into the wading pool again, Xandi?"

"Mama, I'll say, 'Beverly, I don't like it when you are mean to my dolly. You must say you're sorry.' If she doesn't, I'll just bring Buffy home and play with her all alone. Oh, yes, I'll say, 'Good-bye, Beverly' very nicely."

"But Xandi, then she still will probably start calling you 'Ugly Xandi.' "

"I'll say, 'Smiles make everybody beautiful. Do you have a beautiful smile, Beverly? Let's see who can be beautiful the longest!' "

"You remember our plan, Xandi!" Mama said and hugged her tightly. "You know how to make peace."

Xandi gave her mother the biggest smile ever.—F.J.C.

Telltale Trail

Be sure that your sin will find you out. Num. 32:23, NIV.

When I was just a little girl we lived in the country. We didn't get our milk from the store. Instead, we bought milk from our farmer-neighbor and carried it home in shiny pails.

The farmer's cows gave such creamy milk that it tasted too rich to drink. Mom let it sit overnight in big shiny pails. The next morning she skimmed off most of the heavy cream to use for making sweet cream butter or to serve on home-made fruit cobbler. Yummm. We kept the milk and cream in an underground cellar because we didn't have a refrigerator to keep things cold.

One day when we had company visiting, Mom sent me to the cellar to get some cream. I took a long time, and when I came back only a little cream was in the pint jar she'd given me to fill.

"Why, Colleen," Mom said, "what happened to the cream?" I looked at the floor and didn't answer, for I knew I had done something wrong. All of a sudden I felt sorry.

Mom went outside. When she came back she said, "You gave the cream to the kitty, didn't you?"

"How did you know?" I wondered out loud.

Mom led me outside and showed me the crooked cream trail by the path to the cellar. She also told me that Jesus knows when we do wrong even when there isn't a cream trail! When we do wrong, we need to tell Jesus that we're sorry. He will forgive us in an instant—just as Mom forgave me.—C.L.R.

Faith

Blessed are they that have not seen, and yet have believed. John 20:29, KJV.

"Grandma, how do we know that God is in heaven watching us?" Jennifer asked. "How can we tell that Jesus hears our prayers?"

"Do you believe that I love you?"

"Of course, Grandma."

"But you can't see my love, can you?"

"No, but I know that you love me."

"Do you believe that spring will come?"

"Yes, Grandma."

"But all we can see now is snow."

"But spring comes every year, Grandma. You know that!"

"Do you believe that your sunflowers will feed the birds next winter?"

"Yes, Grandma. We grow them in the garden every summer."

"But all they are now is a handful of striped seeds."

"H'mmm."

"Do you believe that someday you will have a little brother or sister?"

"I know I will. Mommy told me so."

"Do you believe that there'll be nice green leaves on the tree in my front yard and sweet-smelling blossoms that will grow into juicy ripe apples?"

"Yes, Grandma, and they'll be sweet and delicious like always. Yum!"

"But right now all they are are teeny brown buds on bare black branches." Grandma gave Jennifer a hug. "Do you believe in gifts and promises?"

"Yes, I do."

"Now do you know how we know that God is in heaven watching over us and that Jesus hears our prayers?"

"Yes, Grandma, yes!"

(Talk about ways you know that God hears your prayers.)—V.L.K.

Be an Example

Be an example for the believers. 1 Tim. 4:12, TEV.

Kathy frowned as she dried the last dish and put it away. Why did Mother always want her to help with dishes? Becky and Jane were already outside playing jump rope.

"All done, Mom," Kathy said. "Now can I go out?"

"After you pick up the toys," Mother said.

Kathy frowned at baby Tim, who was pushing a toy truck across the bright-red floor. Why didn't he pick up his own toys? "But Mom," she began.

"Bu Ma," Tim said, his little face all screwed up in a frown.

"Mom, look at Timmy frown."

Mother smiled a sad smile. "Look in the mirror, Kathy. What do you see?"

"I see me," Kathy said.

Mother nodded. "Now say 'But Mom' the way you just did."

It was easy to remember how she felt about picking up all those toys. "But Mom," Kathy said.

"Now," Mother said, "what do you see?"

"I see me," Kathy answered, "and I'm frowning. But—"

"Baby Tim is like the mirror," Mother said. "He reflects what we put in front of him. That's how he learns—from what he sees us doing."

Kathy thought about that, then she smiled. She said, "I belong to Jesus, so I want to show Timmy good things to learn."

"That's right," Mother said. "You want to be a good example."

Kathy smiled and bent to pick up a ball. Tim reached for a toy truck. "Look, Mom," Kathy cried, "it's working. Timmy is smiling too. And he's helping me."—N.C.P.

Trevor's Rules

I pray that everything may go well with you and that you may be in good health. 3 John 2, TEV.

Trevor pulled on the big gymnasium door. As he walked inside, Trevor spotted Dad pulling out the blue, spongy mats. "Come on, son," Dad called. "Let's see your forward roll." Since Dad was a gymnastics coach, Trevor got to work out as often as he wanted to.

Quickly Trevor took off his shoes. Then he put his hands on the mat, tucked in his head, and rolled over. Trevor just loved doing gymnastics.

Next, Dad lay on the mat holding firmly to Trevor's arms. With Dad's help, Trevor flung his feet up in the air. Over and over Dad and Trevor practiced. Trevor listened carefully as Dad told him exactly what to do.

Trevor hopes to be a very good gymnast someday. Can you guess what his dad told him is the most important thing he can do? He said, "Trevor, to be a good gymnast, you must always keep your body strong and healthy."

Here are Trevor's good health rules:

1. Eat good food, including lots of fruits and vegetables. But eat only at the right times.

2. Exercise out in the fresh air and sunshine each day.

3. Drink plenty of water each day.

4. Get lots of good sleep.

5. Don't ever use harmful things like cigarettes, alcohol, or drugs.

6. Always love and trust God with a happy heart.

If you want to be strong and healthy, begin following these good health rules today. You'll be glad you did!—P.M.M.

Andy, the Parrot—
A Mission Story

The Lord is my strength and song, and He has become my salvation. Ps. 118:14, NKJV.

Andy the parrot wanted to fly. Being a parrot, he was born to fly. But Andy the parrot could not fly. Andy's owner had his wings cut short to keep him from flying away.

Each day Andy would climb up the jambolana tree and sit on the tallest branch. He'd look around and listen, and whistle to the other birds. Then he'd flap his wings as if he were getting ready to fly.

One day while Andy was sitting high up in his usual spot, flapping his short wings, he heard another parrot calling. Andy got excited! He whistled loudly to the other bird, and the bird whistled back. Andy started flapping his wings wildly—turning his head back and forth, preparing to fly. The more the other parrot whistled, the faster Andy flapped his wings. Andy wanted to fly! So he spread his short wings, leaped into the air, and off he went. Zoom, straight down to the ground! What a disappointment. Andy found out that he couldn't fly.

Disappointments come to everybody. You have probably been disappointed before. Maybe your brother promised to take you to the park and he didn't keep his word. Or you were promised a special birthday present and didn't receive it. Try not to be angry or to let the disappointment make you sad. This may be hard to do, but with Jesus' help you can be happy even when disappointments come. Just like the Bible says, Jesus can be your strength and your song.

(Think back to when you were a child and of a time you were disappointed. Tell your child about it, and talk about ways to be happy despite it.)—C.B.T.

Eli's Garden

Man shall not live by bread alone. Matt. 4:4, KJV.

Eli helped Sara pick up rocks while Beth and Pete raked the new garden. When they were finished, Daddy held out a box filled with seed packets.

"You can each choose a vegetable to plant and tend yourselves."

Beth chose green beans, Pete grabbed the cucumber seeds, and Sara reached for the carrots. Eli looked at the seed packets for a long time. He wished there was something he liked. At last he reached for a plain white packet.

"What's this?" Eli asked.

"Sweet peas," Daddy answered.

"I like peas," said Eli. "Do they grow tall?"

"Yes, very tall," said Daddy. "But you can't—"

Eli didn't listen. "I want these." Clutching the packet to his chest, he ran off to plant them in his row along the fence.

As the weeks passed, Eli watered and weeded his plants. They grew taller and taller. Soon they were covered with pretty soft-colored flowers.

The days were long and hot. One day Beth brought Mother green beans from her garden. Pete picked a fat cucumber. When Sara pulled some tender young carrots for dinner, Eli sat down on the back steps with tears in his eyes.

"My garden is no good," he said. "My sweet peas are never going to grow real peas. They're only flowers, not food."

Mother sat down beside Eli and put her arm around him. "Flowers are like food in a way," she said. "We drink in their beauty with our eyes, and they fill our hearts with joy. I think that's why God made so many different kinds of flowers for us to see and smell."

Eli sniffled. "You do?"

Mother nodded, and Eli jumped to his feet. "Then let's go pick some of my flowers. We can put them on the dinner table."

"I think that's a wonderful idea," Mother said. Eli took her hand, and they started for the garden.—M.H.D.

Jesus Knows

He closely watches everything that happens here on earth. Ps. 11:4, TLB.

"Don't go far from the house," Mommy said as she buttoned Mike's coat. "You could get lost in the woods."

Daddy, Mommy, and Mike lived on the edge of a big beautiful woods. Mike didn't want to go far. He didn't want to get lost.

He walked a little way until he saw a big black bird. The bird said, "Caw, caw, caw," and flew to another tree. Mike followed the big bird. Soon it sat on a tree limb and said,

"Caw, caw, caw." Then it flew to another tree, then another. After a while Mike didn't see the bird anymore, so he decided he'd better go home. He started walking.

He walked and walked, but he didn't see his house. He walked some more. Still he couldn't find his way home. After a long time he sat down on a log and cried. He cried and cried, then wiped his face and got up to walk some more. But no matter how far he walked, he was still in the woods. Mike got so tired that he curled up on the ground and cried himself to sleep.

Mike woke up when he felt someone pick him up. He opened his eyes and saw Daddy's happy face. "I was lost," Mike sobbed. "I didn't know where I was."

Daddy's strong arms held him closer. "I didn't know where you were either," he said. "I looked everywhere. But when I asked Jesus to help me, He led me straight to you."

Jesus is always helping us like that. Aren't you glad He always knows where you are?—V.W.

Pointing Fingers

A friend loves at all times. Prov. 17:17, NIV.

Marilyn loved to have her cousins come to visit. But when it rained for three days in a row and they couldn't play outdoors, everyone—including Marilyn—was in a bad mood. The cozy home Marilyn and her parents lived in just wasn't big enough to hold three extra people!

Before long, the visiting cousins got bored. They'd seen Marilyn's pets, watched TV, played games, and talked. Now they needed to get outside and run.

"I wish we could go home," Karen said. She looked around Marilyn's small room and sniffed. "My room at home is much bigger than this."

"So's mine," Jamie put in.

"Mine, too." Even though little Sally didn't half understand what they were talking about, she had to get in on the conversation.

"I like my room." Marilyn looked at the pretty curtains Mom had made, and the matching bedspread. "I don't care if it isn't as big as yours."

"Our TV's bigger too," Jamie said.

Marilyn lost her temper. "Then why don't you just call Uncle Bill and Aunt Jane and have them come get you?" That started a big quarrel. The children began pointing their fingers at each other and yelling, "You started the argument."

"You did."

"No, you did."

Dad came down the hall and stopped at the open door. "Kids, look at your hands. When you point a finger of blame at someone, *three other fingers point back at you*." All four children looked at each other, laughed, and played happily after that.—C.L.R.

A Lucky Girl

I never cease to give thanks for you when I mention you in my prayers. Eph. 1:16, REB.

"Happy Mother's Day!" Lakesha shouted. She handed Mama the card she had made at school.

"This is beautiful!" Mama exclaimed. "All my favorite things are on it—birds, rainbows, and best of all, a picture of you." She touched Lakesha's nose.

At bedtime Mama came in to listen to Lakesha's prayers.

Lakesha ended with "Thank You, God, for a wonderful mother on Mother's Day. I'm so lucky to have her. Amen."

"I'm lucky to have you, too," Mama said. She thought a moment as she stroked Lakesha's hair. "Shall we say a prayer for your first mother on Mother's Day?" she asked. Lakesha was adopted, and she knew Mama was talking about the woman she had been born to.

Lakesha frowned and fell back on her pillow. She folded her arms. "Why should we?" she said angrily. "My first mother didn't love me. She never gave me anything."

Mama took Lakesha's hand. "Your first mother loved you very much, and she gave you a lot."

"No!" Lakesha interrupted. "She just gave me away."

"She gave you a chance," Mama said. "She knew she couldn't take care of you, and she wanted you to have the best. She loved you so much that I got you. That takes a special kind of love from a special kind of lady. I'm thankful to her."

Lakesha looked up at her mother. "Are you sure?" she asked.

Mama nodded. "Absolutely positive!"

Lakesha folded her hands again and closed her eyes. "Thank You, God, for two wonderful mamas on Mother's Day. I'm so lucky to have them. Amen."

Mama smiled. "Amen," she whispered.—V.L.K.

Don't Boast

Whoever wants to boast must boast of what the Lord has done. 1 Cor. 1:31, TEV.

"My bike's newer than yours," Jimmy said, patting the bright red bike that had been his birthday present.

Tom frowned. "Yeah, well, I can ride better than you, and next year I'll have a new bike."

"Oh, yeah?" Jimmy asked.

"Say, Jimmy," Grandpa called from the porch where he was shelling peas. "Come up here for a minute. And bring that fellow with you."

Jimmy started toward the porch. He liked being at Grandpa's for the summer. Grandpa always had good stories and riddles to tell.

"Nice bike," Grandpa said to Jimmy.

Jimmy smiled. "Yeah, it's better than—"

"Get you there any faster?" Grandpa asked.

"No, but—"

"Does it make you a better kid?" Grandpa asked. This sounded like one of Grandpa's riddles.

"No." Jimmy watched the peas fall into the pan.

Grandpa looked up, his eyes twinkling. "It's not a good thing to boast, boys. Makes people mad at each other. Look at the two of you."

Jimmy looked at Tom. He didn't like being mad at his friend.

"If you have to boast," Grandpa went on, "do it about something worthwhile."

"But what would that be, Grandpa?"

Grandpa smiled. "Look around. What do you see?"

Jimmy looked. "I see our house and trees and Mom's flowers."

"And you," Tom said. "And us."

Two peas fell into the pan. "And peas," Jimmy said.

"Where'd it all come from?" Grandpa asked.

Tom looked puzzled, but Jimmy knew. "From God!" he cried. "It all comes from God!"

Grandpa smiled his biggest smile. "Right, boys. So if you're going to boast, boast about what God's done for us. Now, that's something terrific."

Can you think of some nice things God has done for you?— N.C.P.

Dusty

The Lord is good to all; he has compassion on all he has made. Ps. 145:9, NIV.

"Can we keep her, Mom?" Brandon asked, watching the brown, short-haired dog lying on the patio.

"Yeah, can we?" younger brother Zachery joined in.

"Now, boys, it's not that simple," Mom answered. "Whoever left the dog here must have mistreated her. She's so afraid that she won't let any of us even pet her. She'll need to become friendlier if we're going to keep her."

The boys called her Dusty. They left fresh water outside and fed her each day. Little by little Dusty let the boys come closer.

One day Brandon ran in the house shouting, "Dusty let me pet her! Dusty let me pet her! Now can Dusty be our dog forever?"

Dad and Mom smiled at each other. "Now, that's a wonderful idea," Dad said. "But let me tell you one thing," he added. He was using his deep, important-sounding voice. "Always be kind to Dusty, and she will always trust you."

Today the boys and Dusty are best of friends. Wherever the boys play, Dusty is nearby. If a stranger comes up to the boys, Dusty growls and curls her lip. Dusty loves and trusts her family and wants to protect them.

Aren't you glad God created pets? A furry cat or a playful dog can be so much fun. But you must remember that God expects us to be kind to animals.

Can you think of some ways you can be kind to pets?— P.M.M.

Susie

But we shall all be changed—in a moment, in the twinkling of an eye. 1 Cor. 15:51, 52, NKJV.

"I'd give anything if I could just walk and run like the other children," 12-year-old Susie cried to her mother. "I wish I didn't have to sit in this old wheelchair every day. Will I ever walk?"

Mom knelt by the wheelchair. "Susie, one day you'll be able to walk," she said softly. Susie had been born with a disease called cerebral palsy. Her legs were too weak to hold her, and her foot was twisted. Susie had had an operation in her left hip, and now she had to use a wheelchair or crutches to get around.

But being in a wheelchair didn't stop Susie from going to the store or to church. She loved Jesus and believed that one day she'd be able to walk—without crutches. One day she would not have to sit in a wheelchair all day long.

She kept on praying, "Please, Jesus, help me to walk."

One day the doctor said, "Susie, how would you like for me to operate on your foot to see if we can straighten it?"

Susie was so happy. *Maybe I'll be able to walk like other children*, she thought.

Susie had the operation, and her foot was straightened. Now she can stand on her feet even without crutches, and she's looking forward to growing stronger so she won't have to use her wheelchair. But more important, Susie is looking for Jesus to come soon. She wants to thank Him in person for helping her walk.—C.B.T.

Hand of Friendship

The good treasure of [the] heart brings forth good. Luke 6:45, NKJV.

Jessica hurried into the day-care center with her mother. She looked around for her friend Maggie. There was a new girl standing near the door with her coat on. She was tiny like Jessica. But her hair wasn't curly and blonde. It was straight and shiny black. And her eyes were red, for she had been crying.

"I'll pick you up right after work," Mommy promised, giving Jessica a hug and a kiss. Jessica waved good-bye and went to hang up her coat.

"Come see the new blue fish," Maggie called when she saw her. Jessica ran over to the fish tank and they watched the fish swimming around. "There's a new girl over by the door," Jessica said after a few minutes.

"I know," said Maggie, still watching the fish. "Her name is Mei. She doesn't know very many words. And she won't come and play." Maggie turned away. "Let's go play in the playhouse now."

Jessica started to follow, then stopped. The new girl was still standing by the door. She looked so sad and lonely. Jessica remembered how scared she felt when she was new. She walked over to Mei and said, "Hi. Do you want to come play with me?"

Mei shook her head. "Mother go away. I wait here. She come back."

"Did she go to work?" Jessica asked. Mei nodded.

"It will be a long time before she comes back," Jessica told her. "But don't worry. She'll come for you, and I'll be your friend. We can have lots of fun together."

"Friend." Mei smiled a shy smile. "Mei like be friends," she said.

"Come on. Hang up your coat. Then I'll show you the fish. They're blue." Jessica took Mei's hand, and they hurried across the room.—M.H.D.

We Must Do Our Part

Your spirit wants to do what is right, but your body is weak. Mark 14:38, ICB.

Jaime had a problem. He was too chubby, so he was on a diet. A diet is a special program for eating less food and eating less often. Already Jaime had lost enough weight so that his mother had taken in the waist of his blue jeans. He could even run faster!

Jaime's mother had been helping him remember this program. But tomorrow Jaime was going to begin nursery school.

"Who in nursery school will keep me from eating more than I need?" Jaime asked in a very little voice. "How will I keep from asking for food the other kids don't want, Mommy?"

"Your new teacher will help you, Jaime, and you can help yourself," Mommy said. "Every day we will still talk about the things *you* can do. Let's go over them again. *You* can pray and ask Jesus to help you."

"I can chew my food slowly," Jaime joined in, remembering the program.

"You will feel like you've eaten more and you won't finish eating before everyone else," Mommy added. "And *you* can breathe in deeply through your nose and then puff the air out slowly through your mouth. This will keep you thinking about something else."

Jaime showed Mommy his deep breathing and super puffing.

At the end of a puff Jaime added, "*I* can slowly sip a little water. This will fill the empty spaces in my tummy."

"And *you* can turn in a direction not facing the food until you are allowed to leave the table. If you don't see the food, you won't think about eating as much. Satan plans how to get you to do wrong things."

"And *I* must plan how to do right things!" Jaime shouted and clapped his hands.—F.J.C.

Mom, My Room's Pink!

He has made everything beautiful in its time. Eccl. 3:11, NIV.

When Betty, Billy, and their mother moved from California to Washington, the children didn't know if they'd like their new home. Sure, it was great to be close to Grandma and Grandpa now that Dad and Mom no longer lived together. But wouldn't the rain ever stop?

Betty stood at her window and looked out into the bare brown branches of a tree that had dropped all its leaves. "In California we have flowers all the time," she complained.

Mom smiled at her daughter. She looked mysterious. "Just wait a few months," she said. "You'll be surprised at what that tree does."

"Really?" Little Billy snuggled up to Mom. "Is it a miracle tree?"

"Not exactly, but God has a lot of beauty in it just waiting for spring and summer."

Betty sighed. How could such a drooping, sad tree ever be beautiful? She wished she could go back to California. The lonely tree made her feel even worse.

Soon the children made new friends at school and church. Betty didn't have so much time just to stare out the window at the tree, so she didn't see what was happening. Then one afternoon she burst into her room and stopped still. Her eyes opened wide. "Mom, come look!" she called. "My room's pink!" Beautiful bright-pink blossoms covered the dogwood tree, and Betty's white-walled bedroom really did look pink. God had made the tree beautiful when it was time, just as He makes us beautiful when we invite Him into our heart.—C.L.R.

Poor Panda!

Love is patient and kind. Love envies no one. 1 Cor. 13:4, REB.

Gunnar watched Mama bathing baby Greta. He put a "pout" on his face. "I wish you loved only me," Gunnar said.

Mama stroked Gunnar's hair. "That wouldn't be right, Gunnar," she said. "A mother has enough love for all her children."

Gunnar went to play with his toy turtle. "Know what, Pacer? I liked it better before my baby sister was born," he told him.

Later when Mama was reading the newspaper, Gunnar noticed a picture of a panda on the back page. "Mama, what's that panda doing?" he asked.

Mama turned the paper over and read the article. "Oh," she said, "that's a mother panda in a zoo far away. She had two babies, but one died."

"Why?" asked Gunnar.

"Because she took care of only one and ignored the other," Mama explained.

"That's terrible," said Gunnar sadly. "Poor baby panda." Suddenly he remembered something. He reached out and gently touched baby Greta's cheek. "Poor panda," he said. "Good thing people are different from pandas. His mama wasn't like our mama. She just didn't know she could love both her children."

Mama pulled Gunnar close. "Right," she said, holding Gunnar in one arm and reaching for baby Greta with the other.—V.L.K.

Don't Listen to Bad People

Evil people listen to evil ideas. Prov. 17:4, TEV.

"Come on," Danny said, "it'll be easy. He won't catch us."

Jack frowned. "Someone might get hurt," he said.

Danny made a face. "Nah. It'll just be fun. What's the matter? You scared or something?"

Jack didn't answer right away. He wasn't exactly scared. He just had a funny feeling in the bottom of his stomach. It was a feeling he didn't like.

He got back on his bike. "I've got to go now," he said. "It's time for supper."

Danny nodded. "See you afterward. Then we'll fix old man Smithers. We'll fix him good."

Jack rode off toward home. He didn't like Mr. Smithers either. No one liked him, because he was always yelling at everyone. But what Danny wanted to do was bad.

At home Jack washed his hands and went to help Mother set the table for supper. "You're awfully quiet," his mom said.

Jack frowned. "I guess I'm thinking."

Mother started dishing up the chili. "Want to talk about it?"

Jack nodded. Maybe Mom would help him figure this out. "It's Danny. He wants to go trash old Mr. Smithers' yard."

Mom put a bowl of chili on the table. "And he wants you to go with him?"

Jack nodded. He waited, but Mother didn't say any more. Finally he went on. "Mr. Smithers is mean. He yells and chases us away."

Mother sighed. "There *are* mean people in the world," she said.

"But it still isn't right, is it?" Jack asked.

"What do you think?"

Jack took a deep breath. "Being mean to Mr. Smithers won't make him nicer. And I don't think Jesus wants us to be mean to anyone. So I'm not going to go with Danny."

Mother smiled and gave Jack a big hug. "I'm proud of you. You know better than to listen to kids who want to do bad things."

What should you do when someone tries to get you to do something naughty?—N.C.P.

Something to Hold On to—A Mission Story

Do not be afraid—I am with you! I am your God—let nothing terrify you! I will make you strong and help you; I will protect you and save you. Isa. 41:10, TEV.

The road ended. We parked the jeep and started walking to the village far away. We were going to tell these people that Jesus loved them.

We were in the jungles of Borneo. Here the woodland trail crossed many streams. Building bridges in Borneo is easy, but crossing them is very hard. The people cut bamboo poles or small trees long enough to go from one bank to the other. With their bare feet they can easily cross over the shaky logs. But I couldn't do it. I was too scared.

I looked down at the muddy water. There was nothing to hold on to. Only one narrow log crossed the stream, and I was afraid. That shaky bridge stood in my way. I could not join the others to bring Jesus to that heathen village. I knew I would fall into the water below. Oh, how I wanted something to hold on to!

Then my husband had an idea. "Hold on to my belt," he said. "I'll walk carefully, and you can follow me." I trusted him. And so, holding on very tight, I followed just behind. Now it was easy!

Jesus wants you to follow Him all the way to heaven. When you obey your parents and are kind to others, you are following Jesus.—E.E.L.

Beggar or Angel?

Do not forget to entertain strangers, for by so doing some have unwittingly entertained angels. Heb. 13:2, NKJV.

Sabbath dinner was over, and everyone was full. Grandmother was taking the dishes off the table when she heard a knock at the front door.

Little Doris and her cousin, Jean, ran to open the door, and there stood a tall, kind-looking man. His clothes were old but clean. The two girls looked up at the man and asked him what he wanted. "Please. Can you give me something to eat?" he asked.

Doris ran to the kitchen to tell Grandmother that a beggar was at the door and he was hungry. Grandmother stopped cleaning off the table and came to the front door.

"May I help you, sir?" asked Grandmother.

"Yes, ma'am," said the man. "Would you give me something to eat?"

"Our family has just finished eating dinner," Grandmother said. "But I will try to find something good for you."

The kind-looking gentleman smiled. "I know this is your Sabbath and you don't cook," he said. "If you will just give me a cup of Postum, that will be fine."

Doris and Jean watched the man while their grandmother went to the kitchen to fix him the Postum. Soon Grandmother returned with a nice hot cup. She asked the man if he wanted to come inside the house and drink the

Postum. He said, "No." He said that he would sit on the floor outside the door in the hallway of their apartment house.

The girls and their grandmother watched the man as he drank the Postum. When he had finished, he got up, and as he handed the cup to Grandmother he said, "May God bless you and your house." Then he turned and walked down the hallway toward the outside door.

Doris and Jean raced inside the apartment and ran to the living room window so they could see the man when he came out the front door. They waited and they waited—but he never came out.

"Grandmother," said Doris, "the man hasn't come out yet." Grandmother looked at her two granddaughters and said, "Doris and Jean, that was no ordinary man. I believe that was an angel sent by God."

The girls looked at each other and whispered, "An angel?"

"Yes," said Grandmother with a big smile. "I think he came to check up on me. We must be careful to treat people kindly," she said, "because we could be entertaining angels from heaven."

With a thoughtful look on her face, and speaking to no one in particular, Grandmother said softly, "Yes, I think he came to check up on me."—C.B.T.

A Time to Share

Judge not, that you be not judged. Matt. 7:1, RSV.

Danny was playing with his blocks when Daddy brought a boy into his room. The boy had a little red truck in his hand.

"This is Jamie," Daddy said. "He's come to play with you." Then Daddy closed the door.

Jamie put his truck by the door and sat down beside Danny. "Blocks are fun to play with," he said.

Danny frowned. *Jamie might not know how to play nice with blocks*, he thought. "Mine," Danny said, and guarded the blocks with his arm.

Jamie went over to the toy shelf and took down an airplane. "This is fun to play with," he told Danny.

Danny jumped up in alarm. Jamie might break his airplane. "Mine!" He ran over and grabbed the airplane, then hurried back to guard his blocks. Each time Jamie took a toy from the shelf, Danny jumped up and snatched it away. Soon Danny was surrounded by toys and the shelf was empty.

Suddenly Jamie had an idea. He picked up his own truck. "Mine," he said and pushed the truck over to Danny.

Danny looked surprised. "Yours," he said and gave the truck a shove.

Jamie pushed it back again.

Soon the little truck was racing back and forth. Both boys laughed. *Jamie knows how to play nice with toys*, Danny thought.

"Let's build a road and a bridge with my blocks," said Danny. They were just getting started when the door opened.

"Time to go, Jamie," Daddy said. Jamie picked up his truck and waved good-bye.

Danny waved too. He was sorry he'd wasted so much time worrying about his toys getting broken. Toys are more fun to play with when you share them with a friend.— M.H.D.

Judi Gets Skates

Unless you . . . become as little children, you will never get into the Kingdom of Heaven. Matt. 18:3, TLB.

Five-year-old Judi had wanted roller skates for a long time. Finally she stood in the store with Mommy, looking at all the different colors of skates. She looked at white skates with bright-pink laces and wheels. She looked at black skates with neon-green laces and wheels. She looked at lavender skates with purple laces and wheels. How could she ever choose?

Finally Judi smiled. "I'll take the lavender ones," she said. Then she sat right down on the floor and started looking them over. She looked inside the soft leather tops. She looked at the bright-purple laces. She turned the skates over and slowly turned the purple wheels.

Finally she looked up at Mommy. "Where are the little motors that make them go?" she asked.

Mommy laughed and snatched Judi into her arms. "Oh, honey," she said, "motors don't make skates go. Strong little legs make them fly like the wind."

Judi felt bad because she didn't know. She felt dumb. But do you know what Jesus said? He said everyone has to become like little children to go into heaven. So don't ever feel bad if you don't know things. No one knows everything. And Jesus loves little children best of all.—V.W.

Squirrels and Blue Jays

When times are good, be happy. Eccl. 7:14, NIV.

Just outside our patio door is a cement strip, two steps leading down into the yard, and a planter filled with flowers. Big shrubs hide part of the cedar fence between our home and our neighbors. Huge maple trees give shade in spring and summer and wonderful colored leaves in the fall.

But the best thing about our backyard is our visitors! Not people visitors, but animal visitors. Many kinds of birds sing in the trees and swoop down to the birdbath that we keep filled with fresh water. Not only do the robins and blue jays and others come for a bath, but a family of gray squirrels and some neighborhood cats use it for a drinking fountain!

Every day Mom and I put out food for the squirrels. Two big black crows sit in the trees and go "caw caw." The squirrels come right up to our glass door and sit there eating their breakfast. They hold pieces of food in their paws and sit up on their back legs.

The blue jays are real robbers. They like to zoom down and snatch pieces of bread crust, peanuts, and other squirrel goodies. Then the squirrels scold and the blue jays screech.

Little Becky can't understand why they don't get along better. "There's enough food for all of them," she says. "Why do they fight?"

Becky is right. They should be happy, for times are good. We need to remember the squirrels and blue jays. We need to be happy, too, just as the Bible tells us.—C.L.R.

Light a Candle

You are light for all the world. . . . Like the lamp, you just shed light among your fellows, so that, when they see the good you do, they may give praise to your father in heaven. Matt. 5:14-16, REB.

Sibby looked sad. He told Aunt Theresa, "Our Sabbath school teacher said, 'Light a candle for someone this month.' But you know I'm not allowed to light any fire."

Aunt Theresa explained, "Lighting a candle the way your teacher meant it doesn't have anything to do with real fire. Sometimes grown-ups talk in symbols. A symbol stands for something else. 'Lighting a candle' means doing something really special for someone to brighten that person's life."

"Really?" Sibby said. "What can I do?"

"Don't worry," Aunt Theresa said. "When you see someone having a dark time, you'll know what to do to light the flame."

But weeks passed, and Sibby worried. He hadn't found any dark spots to brighten.

One morning his elderly neighbor fell and broke her hip. Sibby watched the ambulance take Mrs. Morsicato away. He got out paper and crayons and drew her a get-well card full of love. Then he picked some wildflowers. Mama took the card and flowers to Mrs. Morsicato at the hospital.

One day Sibby remembered. "Oh no, Aunt Theresa, what am I going to do? I haven't lit a candle for anybody yet!"

"Oh, you haven't?" Aunt Theresa said with a smile. She handed Sibby a card.

It said:

Dearest Sibby, Thank you for the beautiful get-well card. What a lovely surprise! And how did you know wildflowers are my favorites? You really know how to make the dark moments bright! Love, Mrs. Moriscato.

Sibby's eyes sparkled. "You mean I lit a candle?" he gasped.

Aunt Theresa beamed. "Bright as bright can be!"— V.L.K.

Look at the Heart

But the Lord said to him . . . "Man looks at the outward appearance, but I look at the heart." 1 Sam. 16:7, GNB.

Jeremy turned the pages in the magazine. "Look, Mom," he said. "Isn't this a pretty house?"

Mom leaned over the arm of her chair to look. "You're right. It's a very pretty house."

After a minute Jeremy asked, "Why isn't our house this pretty?"

"Don't you think it is?" Mom asked.

Jeremy shook his head.

"You know," Mom said, "the inside of that house may not be as pretty as the outside. You can't always tell about the inside of things from looking at the outside." She smiled. "Our church is a plain building, but it's very nice inside."

Jeremy thought about that. "You're right. I feel real good in there."

"Remember the apple you had the other day?" Mom asked. "The red shiny one?"

He made a face. "I remember. It was real pretty, but there was a worm inside."

"People are a lot like buildings and apples," Mom went on. "You can't tell about the inside by looking at the outside."

Jeremy frowned. "That's like my teacher," he said. "Mrs. Jackson's skin is all wrinkled, but she's a real nice person."

Mom nodded. "That's right."

"I'll remember," Jeremy said. "From now on I'm going to think about what people are like on the inside. That's what's important." —N.C.P.

The Shared Lunch— A Story From the Bible

There is a boy here who has five loaves of barley bread and two fish. But they will certainly not be enough for all these people. John 6:9, TEV.

The sun peeked in the window of the small room awaking a young boy. He yawned and stretched his arms. *What was all that noise in the street?* he wondered. The young boy listened carefully. That sounded like his neighbors talking.

"I hear that teacher-healer called Jesus is down by the lake," a man shouted. "He tells wonderful stories. Why don't you come along?"

"Think I will . . ." But that is all the young boy heard. Quickly he dressed and ran to Mom, who was busy baking barley cakes. "Could I go to the lake and listen to the teacher Jesus?" the young boy begged.

Mom thought it was a wonderful idea, but insisted her boy take a lunch since the day would be long. After many hours the five loaves and two fishes would taste good!

Jesus' stories were so wonderful the little boy did not even think about his lunch until almost evening. He wouldn't have thought of it then, but a big man asked if he'd mind sharing his lunch. The man said that Jesus needed his lunch.

Do you remember the rest of the story? Jesus blessed those five loaves and two fishes. That small shared lunch fed 5,000 men, not counting women and children—all because a young boy shared.

Do you have the "sharing habit"? Do you happily share your toys? a treat? your swing set? Jesus still blesses children today who share with a happy heart!

(Talk about times you shared or someone shared with you.)—P.M.M.

Little Green Apples

Take and eat it; and it will make your stomach bitter, but it will be as sweet as honey in your mouth. Rev. 10:9, NKJV.

"Oh, my stomach hurts," wailed Lisa, holding her hands tightly against her stomach, as if by holding her stomach she would stop the pain.

Those little green apples had looked so tempting, and they had tasted so good. Mother had said not to eat the green apples as they were not ripe yet. *But*, thought Lisa, *the apples couldn't be that bad. I'll just try one.* The first green apple was a bit sour—but good. Lisa tried another green apple, and then another one, until she had eaten five green apples. By the time she had eaten the fifth apple, Lisa's stomach was hurting something awful. Lisa sat down on the porch steps, holding her stomach. Now she was sorry she hadn't listened to Mother and had eaten the little green apples.

Soon Mother came outside to see what Lisa was doing. Mother found her sitting on the steps with her head down, crying softly. Tears were trickling down her face. How her stomach ached!

"Lisa, what's the matter, dear?" Mother asked. "Why are you crying?"

"Oh, Mother," cried Lisa, "my stomach hurts."

Mother put her arm around Lisa's shoulder. "Lisa, did you eat some of those green apples?" Lisa could only nod her head up and down—yes, she had.

"Poor Lisa," said Mother. "I'm sorry you're not feeling well. I'm also sorry that you didn't listen to me when I told you the apples weren't ready to eat."

Lisa looked up at Mother. "I'm sorry that I disobeyed you."

Mother gave her a big hug. "I forgive you. Now let's go inside and see what we can do for that stomachache. You'll be better soon."

After taking some medicine, Lisa curled up on her bed for the rest of the afternoon. She hugged her tummy and asked Jesus to forgive her, too. She asked Jesus to help her to be more obedient. After that awful day, Lisa remembered that everything that looks good may not always be the best thing to eat. And that it is best to listen to Mother.—C.B.T.

I'm Going to Get You, Tyler!

Do not say, "I will repay evil." Prov. 20:22, RSV.

Harry made a big red valentine heart for his mother. This time he didn't smear the paste. And the lace doily was white and clean. Harry had a happy smile as he carefully picked up the heart at the top with both hands and started back to his desk.

Tyler, sitting in front of him, turned around. He looked at the heart.

"That's ugly," Tyler said. He grabbed Harry's wrists and pulled his hands apart.

The heart ripped right in two. Tyler laughed and ran to the back of the room.

Harry dropped the heart into the wastebasket and went back to his seat. He'd brought extra valentines from home in case he forgot somebody. He could give Mom one of those. But it wasn't the same.

"I'm going to get you, Tyler!" Harry muttered between tight teeth.

All through lunch Harry tried to think of something mean to do to Tyler.

It wasn't easy. Tyler had already thought up all the mean things to do.

After the last recess Mrs. Westly told the children to put the paper bags they'd decorated to hold valentines on their desks. Then she told them to pass out their valentines. All the bags were filling up. Except one. Tyler's bag was still empty.

Now I know what I'm going to do to Tyler, Harry thought. He got out his extra valentines. He found the right one and signed it. Then he wrote Tyler's name on the envelope. When Tyler wasn't looking, Harry dropped it into his bag.

Tyler held the valentine in his hand for a long time before he opened it. It said, "Let's be friends." Tyler looked at Harry and held up the valentine. Harry nodded. Then Tyler did something Harry had never seen him do before.

He smiled.—M.H.D.

Julie's Turtle

Always keep on praying. 1 Thess. 5:17, TLB.

"Mommy, Pokey's gone!" Julie cried. Mommy and Julie looked everywhere for Julie's turtle. But they couldn't find him.

That night Julie prayed for Jesus to keep Pokey safe and bring him home.

But Pokey didn't come home. Julie pleaded with God. "Please bring Pokey back to me before he gets hurt." Still Pokey didn't come.

"The Bible tells us to keep praying," Mommy said.

So Julie prayed every day for Pokey. When he didn't come home, she felt sad. "Maybe Jesus doesn't love me," she told Mommy. "Or Pokey."

"Yes, He does," Mommy said. "He does so many things to show that He loves you. Even if Pokey doesn't come home, you can know Jesus cares. But keep praying."

Julie kept praying. One day a girl stood on Julie's porch and took a big turtle from a box. "I found this turtle in our backyard," she said. "A girl down the street said it's yours."

She barely got the words out before Julie grabbed the turtle and hugged it to her. "Jesus heard my prayer," she squealed. "Did you know that? He answered my prayer to bring back Pokey. I thought He didn't care about turtles, but He does!" She turned her face right up to the sky. "Thank You, Jesus," she called.

Aren't you glad that God loves us enough to hear our prayers? Even when they're about a big green turtle? — V.W.

"Lost" Is a Scary Word

O Lord, come quickly to help me. Ps. 70:1, NIV.

Jeremy usually did everything Dad said to do. When they went shopping, he stayed close to his father and didn't wander away. Dad had told him how it is easy for little boys to get lost in big stores. So Jeremy always held on to Dad's hand except when Dad had to pay for something.

One day, however, Jeremy saw a great stack of toys just a little way from Dad. "It won't hurt if I go over there," he whispered. "I'll still be able to see Dad, and he has to wait for the clerk to wrap his package."

Jeremy hurried down the aisle to the toy counter. Some of the toys moved. Some of them talked. One toy had lights that flashed and bells that rang when the saleslady wound it up.

Jeremy forgot everything except the toys. But when the woman stopped winding them and moved away, Jeremy remembered Dad. He turned around, but all he could see was a crowd of strangers!

"Dad?" Jeremy called. He turned and looked the other way. A funny feeling in his stomach made him feel sick. Why had he ever left Dad? What should he do?

Jeremy remembered what Dad had taught him. "Say a prayer," he'd said, "then tell a clerk or store guard if we ever get separated." The little boy whispered, "God, please help me get unlost." He opened his eyes and looked for someone to ask for help. Jeremy ended up at the lost child desk, and Dad found him there.

"I'll never do that again," he promised. "Being lost is so scary." Then he thanked God for helping him.—C.L.R.

Hummingbirds

There are varieties of activity, but in all of them and in everyone the same God is active. 1 Cor. 12:6, REB.

Katya was always doing something.

"Can't you ever just sit still?" asked Daddy.

"Busy, busy, busy," said old Mrs. Kellogg next door.

Everyone was always telling Katya to relax. But Katya didn't need to relax. Katya needed to be active.

She loved visiting Grandma Grace, who understood because she was just like Katya.

They filled all the bird feeders with seeds. They weeded the vegetable garden and picked wildflowers from the field out back. They baked cookies and banana bread and read Bible stories and made clothespin-and-tissue-paper butterflies.

They mixed fresh nectar for the hummingbird feeder and quickly put it back on the porch hook, because hummingbirds were Katya's favorites. Sometimes the tiny birds flew near enough so Katya could hear the whirring of their wings.

One day when Mama came to pick her up, Katya told her about their day and everything she and Grandma Grace had done together.

"You must be exhausted," Mama said. "Can't you ever sit still?"

"She's like a hummingbird," said Grandma Grace. "She's tiny and pert and moves like lightning. She flits here and there, spreading a minute's worth of joy and sparkle wherever she goes."

Mama looked at Katya. Then she nodded and smiled. "A hummingbird indeed," she exclaimed. "Get your wings whirring, and we'll go home." — V.L.K.

Be Wise

Being wise is better than being strong. Prov. 24:5, TEV.

Tony didn't like the look in Butch's eyes. Why didn't Butch go away and let him fish alone? Grandpa always said that fishing alone was good for a fellow — that it gave him time to think. Grandpa was downstream, around the bend.

"Let me see inside your tackle box," Butch said. He jerked open the lid. Butch was really big, really strong. Tony didn't know how to stop him.

"Hey! You've got lots of stuff here."

Tony nodded. "Grandpa—" he began.

"Ah, who wants to hear about some old geezer?" Butch laughed. "I'm lots stronger than any old man. Smarter, too."

Tony didn't believe that. Grandpa knew more than anyone. But Butch was big, and he didn't like to have people tell him things.

Tony reached for his tackle box, but Butch reached too. And he knocked it right over. Hooks and lines and sinkers went everywhere.

"Too bad," Butch said with a nasty smile.

Tony swallowed. He knew Butch had knocked the box over on purpose, but he didn't say anything. He just started picking things up.

Butch started too. He grabbed up a whole handful as though he was going to keep them. Then he got a funny look on his face. "Ouch!" he yelled. "Ow! It hurts!"

Butch had a fishhook stuck in his finger! Tony wanted to run off, but when Butch started pulling at the hook, Tony knew what he had to do. "Don't touch it, Butch. That makes it worse. Come on, we'll go get Grandpa to help."

Grandpa dropped his pole and took hold of the fish hook. He worked the hook out and then washed Butch's finger.

Butch looked at Tony, then at Grandpa. "You're really smart," he said. "I tried, but I couldn't pull it out. It hurt too badly. And I'm strong. Real strong."

Grandpa nodded. "That's true. But you didn't need strength here. You just needed to know what to do."—N.C.P.

No Long Lines

No mere man has ever seen, heard or even imagined what wonderful things God has ready for those who love the Lord. 1 Cor. 2:9, TLB.

Eric loved Friday evening supper. The homemade rolls, his favorite soup, and the flickering candles, made it all so special. And tonight there would be time for the family to eat slowly and talk about important things.

"Eric, what is the first thing you want to do when you get to heaven?" Dad asked.

Six-year-old Eric sat quietly for a moment, then answered, "First I would like to sit on Jesus' lap and have Him tell me a story, but . . . " Eric thought for a moment, "if there is a long line, I'll go pick my animals out first."

Mom, Dad, and older brother laughed. Dad assured Eric that long lines wouldn't be a problem in heaven. In fact, there won't be any problems in heaven.

Have you ever imagined what heaven will be like? Great big animals like lions, giraffes, tigers, bears—all so gentle you can ride on their backs. Gorgeous butterflies and birds flying through the air, and you'll fly right along with them. Flowers in bright and dazzling colors—colors you've never even thought of! If you want, you can go swimming in lakes so clear that you can see all the way to the bottom. You won't even be afraid. If you get water in your nose, do you think it will burn like it does on earth?

Maybe there'll be high snow-covered mountains to ski on. Do you think you'll get cold? You'll make new friends from countries like Brazil, Australia, and Africa. Maybe some of your friends will be children who lived in China or Egypt 3,000 years ago. But guess what! You'll all speak the same language.

But Eric is right. The best part of heaven will be meeting Jesus face to face, sitting on His lap, holding his hand, giving Him a hug. I can hardly wait! How about you?

What do you want to do in heaven?—P.M.M.

The Broken Bed

Correct your child, and you will be proud of him. Prov. 29:17, ICB.

Warren and Shana knew they shouldn't be in Mommy and Daddy's bedroom jumping up and down on their bed. Mommy and Daddy were not home, and they'd told the children to stay out of their bedroom. But Warren wanted to practice jumping so he'd know how to jump on the trampoline when he and his sister went back to school. The house was quiet. No one was looking. And Warren and Shana ran into the bedroom and hopped on the bed.

Up and down they jumped. Higher and higher they went. Harder and harder they came down on the bed, until *crack!* The bed broke! Two scared children quickly left the bedroom, closed the door, and quietly waited for their parents to come home.

Warren blamed Shana, and Shana blamed Warren. Mommy and Daddy said they both were wrong and that they must learn to obey. It made their parents feel sad, but both children got a spanking. After their tears were dried, Warren and Shana said they were sorry for disobeying and breaking the bed. They learned that there are good reasons for rules and promised never to jump on beds again.

What are some of the rules in your house?—C.B.T.

Accidents Happen

Forgive, and you will be forgiven. Luke 6:37, NIV.

"I'm never going to play with Amy again!" Jennifer cried as she burst into the kitchen. "She broke Mandy!" Angry tears rolled down Jennifer's cheeks as she held out the doll.

Mother pushed a fern into the flower arrangement she was working on at the table. She reached for the doll. "I know you feel bad, but I'm sure Amy didn't mean to break Mandy."

"Well, I don't care. I hate her! She's not my friend anymore!" Jennifer jerked her arm out of her coat. Her hand hit Mom's flowers, and the vase went crashing to the floor. Jennifer gasped.

"Look what you've done!" Mom scolded. "That was my favorite vase."

"I'm sorry. It was an accident." Jennifer picked up a flower and put it on the table.

"Please, just go to your room while I clean up this mess," Mother said.

Jennifer felt awful as she climbed the stairs. "I didn't mean to do it," she said to herself.

That's what Amy said when she broke Mandy, Jennifer thought. *She must feel awful too.* She stopped in the hall and picked up the phone.

"I'm sorry I got so mad. I know you didn't mean to break Mandy," Jennifer said when Amy came to the phone.

"Can we still be friends?" Amy asked.

"Yes. See you tomorrow." Jennifer felt much better when she hung up.

A few minutes later Mom came upstairs. She gave Jennifer a hug. "I'm sorry I got upset. I know you didn't mean to break my vase," she said.

"You're not mad anymore?" Jennifer asked.

Mom smiled. "Accidents happen," she said, and gave Jennifer another hug.—M.H.D.

Do You Know My Jesus?

How beautiful upon the mountain are the feet of him who brings good news. Isa. 52:7, NKJV.

The Johnsons are having evening worship. Mr. Johnson has just finished reading the story of Jesus' life in the book titled *The Desire of Ages*. Mr. Johnson looks at his sons and says, "Tonight we are going to practice telling a friend about Jesus."

"I can do it!" 4-year-old Todd calls out, waving his hand.

"OK, son, you're on," Dad says.

"I choose Joey, the new kid at day camp," Todd says, brushing his red hair out of his eyes. "Joey has a collie pup named Taffy. At lunchtime I'll ask to see that picture of Taffy that he always carries. Then I'll say, 'Joey, I want you to meet another good friend of mine. His name is Jesus. He helped me find my dog, Prince, when he got lost. I have some story books at home about Jesus. Let's look at them after camp.' "

"Good job!" Dad says, and everyone claps.

"My turn!" 6-year-old Jeremy calls out as he jumps up from his chair. "I choose my friend Victor. He always sings Sabbath school songs to his crippled grandpa. I'll say, 'Victor, guess who else liked to cheer up people by singing to them? When I tell him, he'll stare at me with his big black eyes and say, 'How do you know that about Jesus?' Then I'll tell him about Mrs. White's book."

"Good idea!" Mrs. Johnson says, and everyone claps.

"Dad, I'm glad Mrs. White wrote about when Jesus was a little boy!" Jeremy exclaimed. "And I like telling my friends about Him."

(Note to Parents: "As a Child," the story of Jesus' childhood, is chapter 7 of Ellen G. White's book The Desire of Ages.)—F.J.C.

The Big Huge Dog

O Lord my God . . . save and deliver me from all who pursue [chase] me. Ps. 7:1, NIV.

Jerry loved dogs. Big dogs, little dogs. Black and brown and white dogs. Short dogs and tall dogs. But he did *not* love Bongo, the big huge boxer dog who lived next door to the house Jerry and his family had just moved into. Bongo snuffled along the fence and growled every time Jerry went into his own yard. Even though Jerry could only catch peeks at Bongo through the cracks in the fence, the dog scared him.

"Bongo is very curious because he's been trained as a watchdog," Mom explained. "Mr. Olson said his family got Bongo because they had a break-in last summer. When I welcomed the Olsons to our neighborhood, Bongo came up and licked my hands. And he would probably be even friendlier if he weren't cooped up in that small yard."

This news didn't make Jerry feel much better. He was just glad for the strong fence and the gate that stayed tightly shut.

Then early one morning Jerry ran out to bring in the paper for Mom. He heard galloping feet. A big huge shadow fell across his path. Frightened, Jerry looked toward the neighbor's open gate. He froze. He tried to run, but his feet just wouldn't work. But Mom had taught him always to talk to God when he was in trouble.

"Please, God, save me from Bongo!" Jerry yelled just before Bongo crashed into him. The next moment Jerry lay flat on his back, and a warm tongue was licking his face. The big huge dog was smiling! Jerry had a new friend, and God had heard Jerry's prayer.—C.L.R.

The Peaceful Dove

Blessed are the peacemakers; they shall be called God's children. Matt. 5:9, REB.

Mrs. Harris told her class about the Noah's ark play. "The main character is the peaceful dove," she said. "It's the most important part."

Travis interrupted. "I should play Noah, the ark builder, because I'm the strongest."

"No, you're not," Lenny argued.

"My muscles are bigger!" Grady shouted.

"Maybe we should draw numbers," Marcus suggested, but he didn't think anyone heard.

"I want to be a bear," yelled Cynthia.

"You? You shrimp," Nick teased.

"Am not," Cynthia said.

"Just ignore it," Marcus said, but Cynthia was already sticking out her tongue at Nick.

Carl said, "Amy, the chatterbox, should be a parrot."

He and Jules laughed.

"It's OK," Marcus said, but Amy made a face at them.

"I should be the dove," Madeline said. "I'm the best actress in the whole class."

"Bragger! Bragger!" scolded Ariel.

Mrs. Harris shook her head. She turned out the lights and waited for the class to get quiet. "I'm very disappointed in your actions," she said. "We're doing a play about peace, and you're all at war."

"But when are you going to give out the parts?" Tony was impatient.

"Perhaps someone who is like the peaceful dove should get to play the part," said Mrs. Harris.

Suddenly everyone looked at Marcus.

"The art teacher will help us make your beak and white wings," Mrs. Harris said. Marcus smiled shyly, and his class crowded around to congratulate him.

Why did the teacher choose Marcus to be the peaceful dove? — V.L.K.

As Deep as the Ocean

May you be able to . . . understand . . . how long, how wide, how deep, and how high his love really is; . . . it is so great that you will never see the end of it or fully know it or understand it. Eph. 3:18, 19, TLB.

Matt felt so excited to be at Wallowa Lake that he could hardly stand still. But finally he and Mommy, Daddy, and Chuck got the big red-and-white tent up.

"May we go to the lake now?" Matt asked.

"Sure," Dad said, "let's go." In a few minutes they reached the lake and the paddleboats.

"Here," said the man who took care of the boats. "Let me help you get your life jackets on."

Chuck and Mommy shared one of the little boats, and Matt rode with Daddy.

The boats had pedals to push to make them go. Daddy and Matt pedaled as hard as they could, and soon they were way out on the clear blue lake.

Matt stopped to rest his legs, and looked over the side. "Wow," he said. "I can't even see the bottom of this lake." He looked some more. He looked into the clear water for a long time. "Look, Daddy," he finally said, "it doesn't have a bottom. The water just keeps going down forever."

Daddy smiled at Matt. "It has a bottom, Matt, but it's nearly 200 feet down. You know what it reminds me of? It reminds me of Jesus' love for us. It really does go on forever. There's no end of it."

"I'm glad Jesus loves me forever too. Aren't you? — V.W.

Jesus' Part First

"Bring the whole tithe into the storehouse, that there may be food in my house. Test me in this," says the Lord Almighty. Mal. 3:10, NIV.

"Mom, look. Nana and Papa put a check inside my birthday card. Is that like dollars?" questioned Laura, the birthday girl.

"Yes, Laura. That check is just the same as a $10 bill," Mom explained.

"Just think of all the things I can buy for $10," Laura said.

"Have you thought about giving Jesus His part first?" Mom asked.

"Giving Jesus His part first?" Laura asked. "You mean like the money you and Daddy put in that little envelope?"

"That's right," Mom answered. "We give our tithe because God has told us we should. That part is His. Our offerings we give just because we are especially thankful for all God has done for us.

"And do you know what, Laura? Dad and I have found that the money that we have left goes just as far as if we had kept it all. We believe God especially blesses the dollars that are left."

Dad took the check to the bank and brought back 10 one-dollar bills for Laura. She put a dollar into the little envelope for tithe, and another dollar in the envelope for her offerings.

The next Sabbath as the offering plate came by, Laura put in her tithe envelope. Laura felt happy. She gave Jesus His part first.—P.M.M.

Buttons and Snow

Inasmuch as you did it to one of the least of these My brethren, you did it to Me. Matt. 25:40, NKJV.

It was a cold, cold day. The wind was blowing hard, and the snow was falling fast. Few people were on the street that winter day. But down the street came an old man walking slowly with his head down to keep the wind and snow from blowing into his face. He didn't have gloves for his hands or a hat on his head. His coat wasn't buttoned either.

Jerry was hurrying home from his job at the furniture store when he saw the old man. As the old man came closer, Jerry stopped him and said, "Sir, it's cold, and your coat is unbuttoned. Let me button it for you."

The old man didn't say anything as Jerry started to button his old thin coat. Jerry looked into the man's eyes and saw tears in them. After buttoning the coat, Jerry patted the man's back and continued on his way home.

At dinner that night Jerry told his parents about the old man and how he had buttoned his coat for him.

Daddy said, "Jerry, you did what Jesus would have done. That's what the Bible means in Matthew 25:40 when it says, 'Inasmuch as you did it to one of the least of these My brethren, you did it to Me.' That's what being like Jesus is all about."

That reminds me of a song we sing: "Be like Jesus, this my song, in the home and in the throng; be like Jesus all day long! I would be like Jesus." Boys and girls, let's be like Jesus.—C.B.T.

The Bully

Love your enemies. Matt 5:44, NIV.

"I wish I didn't have to go to school," said David as he trudged along beside his older sister Megan. "Sammy is always picking on me. I hate him."

Megan stepped around a rain puddle. "The Bible says that we should love our enemies," she told him.

David made a face. "Who could love Sammy? He acts rotten!"

"It doesn't mean love him like we love each other," Megan explained.

"It means being nice to someone who isn't nice to you."

"If I get too close he'll hit me," David told her. "Sammy hits everybody. But most of the time he hits me."

"Sammy's sister told me their parents are getting a divorce," said Megan. "Sammy is very unhappy about it. Maybe he feels really bad and wants everybody else to feel bad too." Megan walked as far as the kindergarten room with David.

"Try being nice to Sammy. Maybe he won't pick on you anymore," she said. Then she ran off to join her friends.

David saw Sammy all by himself near the empty slide. He was a lot bigger than David, and he could hit hard. But Sammy did look sort of sad. David looked around to make sure the playground teacher was close by, just in case he needed her. His knees were shaking when he walked over to Sammy.

"Hi," David said. "Do you want to play on the monkey bars with me?"

"Who, me?" Sammy looked surprised.

"We can climb clear up to the top," said David.

"Nobody ever wants to climb to the top," Sammy said. "Let's go."

They played on the monkey bars until the bell rang to go in. David had fun. Sammy didn't smile. But he didn't hit David, either. *Being nice to Sammy really works*, David thought as they hurried to their room. If I keep on being nice to Sammy, maybe he will be my friend.—M.H.D.

The Best Helper

Fear not, for I am with you. . . . I am your God. I will strengthen you; I will help you. Isa. 41:10, TLB.

"Come here, Jenny," Mommy called. "Let me button your coat."

"No!" Jenny said. "I'm big now. I don't need your help anymore." Jenny struggled with the buttons for a long time. Finally she had to ask Mommy to button her coat.

The next day Daddy started to put some jelly on Jenny's toast. "No, Daddy," she said. "I'm big. I can do it myself." But poor Jenny. The knife was too big for her little hand, and she spilled some bright-red raspberry jelly on the tablecloth.

A few days later Jenny asked if she could pour the milk into glasses for lunch. "Be careful," Mommy said. "It's easy to spill."

Jenny pushed a chair up to the breakfast bar and started filling the glasses. But the milk didn't go into the glasses! It went over the edge, and all over the tabletop.

Jenny wanted to be older than she was, didn't she? But no one in the world can do everything. Not even mommies and daddies. Everyone needs help sometimes.

Jesus is our biggest help. And you're never too young or too old to ask for His help. In what ways do grown-ups need help from Jesus? In what ways do you need help?—V.W.

A Funny Kind of Light

You are my lamp, O Lord; the Lord turns my darkness into light. 2 Sam. 22:29, NIV.

Tara and Tom loved going to their great-grandmother's home just outside the big city. Although Nana was more than 80 years old, she still lived in the same house she'd lived in since she was a girl. It had a warm, dry attic filled with chests and trunks of wonderful things to see—old clothes for playing dress-up, pictures, and faded and dried flowers.

Two shiny glass lamps stood on a tall chest of drawers. "Nana, what are those for?" Tom peered all around them. "What good are they? I don't see any switch to turn them on."

Nana laughed. Her face crinkled like her sugary ginger cookies.

"Child, those are oil lamps," she said. She took one down. "See? They're all filled, ready for winter."

"Why, Nana?" Tara asked. "You have electricity." She stared at the funny kind of lamp.

"Sometimes the electricity goes off out here. During the winter I keep these downstairs just in case."

Tom didn't say anything, but he didn't think the oil lamp could give much light. But Tom was wrong.

A few weeks later when the children were spending the night with Nana, the electricity went off. Nana just took off the glass chimneys from the lamps that now sat on the mantel. She turned up the wick, struck a match, lit the wick, and put the chimney back on. Yellow light danced in the room. Even more light came with the second lamp. "The chimneys have to be clean if they're to shine, just as we must keep clean inside to shine for Jesus," Nana said.

Tara and Tom never laughed at the funny lamps again.

What does it mean to be clean inside so you can shine for Jesus?—C.L.R.

A Little Brighter

Always treat others as you would like them to treat you. Matt. 7:12, REB.

Daddy and Jacob talked about the golden rule. "Who gave it to us?" Daddy asked.

"Jesus," Jacob answered.

"Right," Daddy said. "Jesus told us to treat one another just like we would want to be treated. So whenever you're not sure how to act toward someone, put yourself in that person's place."

"OK," said Jacob, still not sure if he would know.

One day Jacob's older brother Todd offered to take him and his friend Stephen kite-flying at the park.

Todd got Jacob's kite off the ground. Jacob and Stephen took turns keeping it high in the air.

Several yards away Jacob spotted another small boy struggling with his kite. Stephen noticed him too. He said, "Look. He'll never get that kite flying alone. We're lucky."

Just then the golden rule popped back into Jacob's head. He pretended he was the little boy having trouble with his kite. He knew how he'd want to be treated. Jacob handed Stephen the string and walked over to the boy.

"Hi. You having trouble?" Jacob asked.

"Sure am. I can't get my kite up," the boy said sadly.

"What's your name?"

"Otis."

"Well, Otis, my big brother's here. He can help. Come on," Jacob said.

Todd helped Otis, and soon two kites danced freely on the wind as four boys laughed together below.

There was nothing like the golden rule to make a shining day even brighter! — V.L.K.

Don't Worry

Do not be worried and upset. John 14:1, TEV.

Peter felt really bad. He wanted to cry, but he didn't want anyone to see that he felt bad. So he went out to his favorite hiding spot, up in the tree house. But being there didn't make him feel better.

He couldn't understand it. Why wouldn't his folks buy him a new bike? Jimmy Cooper had a new bike. A bright-red one with lots of chrome. Bill Jaspers had a new bike too. Peter was the only one who had to ride a rusty old thing that was too small for him.

Peter stared out over the yard. Dad had said they didn't have enough money for a bike. And he'd been frowning. Did that mean they didn't have enough money for other things? Did that mean they'd be like Sue Farini's family, and have to move out of their house? Go to some awful place to live?

Peter didn't know. But he didn't like the funny sick feeling in his stomach. He didn't know much about money, but he knew people had to have some. And if Mom and Dad didn't have enough, he didn't know what they'd do.

Later that night Peter knelt to say his prayers. "Bless Mom and Dad," he said, "and help them have enough money."

When his prayers were over and Mom was tucking him in, she asked, "Peter, why did you pray to God about money?"

Peter sighed. "Dad said there wasn't enough money for a new bike. I got scared. I thought maybe we'd have to leave our house. Like the Farinis did."

Mom grabbed Peter up in a big hug. "It's not like that," she said. "We have enough money for the things we really need. Remember what Jesus told people. 'Do not be worried and upset,' He said. 'Believe in God and believe also in me.'"

"I believe in Jesus," Peter said. He felt better already.

Mom hugged him again. "That's good," she said. "Then you don't have anything to worry about. God will take care of us." She helped him lay back in the bed and pulled the covers up around his neck. "You just go to sleep. God will take care of the rest."—N.C.P.

Afraid

The angel of the Lord encamps all around those who fear Him. Ps. 34:7, NKJV.

Brittany nestled under her warm blankets. Her bed felt so soft and snuggly. But Brittany was not happy. Brittany was afraid. The wind howled outside, her curtains blew over her bed, and when she peeked her eyes open, the shadows chased around her wall.

"Mama . . . Mama," Brittany called timidly. After what seemed a long time, Brittany heard the swishing sound of Mama's slippers against the carpet as she walked into the bedroom.

"I'm so scared," Brittany whispered with a soft sob.

"Why are you afraid?" Mama asked kindly.

"Well, something is thumping on the roof, and hear that 'howlie' sound. And Mama, why are those shadows running up and down my wall?"

"Honey, I think it is all because of the wind. The wind is making the branch hit the roof, and it's the wind that is howling. The shadows on your wall are from the branches swaying back and forth."

"Do you know what I think would help you feel better?" Mama questioned. "Let's ask God to send His angels to surround your bed and to surround our house so you don't have to be afraid."

After that scary night, each evening Mama would pray her special angel prayer for Brittany. Now Brittany could go to sleep without being afraid.—P.M.M.

Denny and the Five Dollars

Little children, let no one deceive you. He who practices righteousness is righteous, just as He is righteous. 1 John 3:7, NKJV.

Little Denny was playing in the street in front of his house. He was skipping, hopping, kicking stones, having a good time playing by himself when he looked down and there in the street he saw some money.

He quickly picked up the money and hurried into the house to the kitchen, where Mother was cooking dinner. "Mother, Mother, look what I found. A dollar bill."

Mother took the money from little Denny and saw that it was not a one-dollar bill, but a five-dollar bill. Smiling, Mother said, "Denny, this is a five-dollar bill. That's a lot of money. Where did you find it?"

Denny was so excited! "In the street," he said. "I found the money in the street. It's mine, isn't it? Can I keep the money?"

Mother looked at the money, then she looked at Denny. "Denny," said Mother, "we must try to find the person who lost this. I'm going to put the money in this jar on the shelf, and then Daddy and I will ask some of the people who live on our street if they lost it. If no one has lost it, then the money will be yours. But you can't have the money until we've talked to all the people and made sure it doesn't belong to any of them.

Two weeks went by, and the money was still in the jar while Mother and Daddy talked with the people about the lost five dollars.

Finally Mother came to Denny and said, "Denny, Daddy and I have talked with many people, and they all said that they did not lose the money."

"Now the money is mine," said Denny happily.

"Yes," said Mother, "the money is yours. You were an honest little boy, waiting to see if the person who had lost the money would come get it. Now you may buy something with it."

With the help of Mother and Daddy, Denny bought a nice set of Bible story books. Denny is a grown man now, and he still has the Bible books that were bought with the five dollars. And when Denny thinks about finding the money and waiting to see if anyone would come to claim it, he knows that being honest is the best way.

Can you think of times that you have been honest?—C.B.T.

A New Friend for Joey

Thou shalt not steal. Matt. 19:18, KJV.

Joey sat on the front step with his chin in his hands. There was no one to play with since Bobby moved away. Then he saw a little brown pup with floppy ears trotting down the street. Joey ran down the walk and opened the gate.

"Hi, fella," Joey called. The puppy ran over and jumped on him. Joey bent down to pet him. The puppy was wearing a new red collar. He licked Joey's face and Joey laughed. He pretended not to see the collar.

"You must be a stray," he said. "Want to come play with me?"

The puppy followed Joey into the backyard. He barked as they ran around the lawn.

Mother came outside to see what the noise was about. "Where did that puppy come from?" she asked.

"He's a stray," said Joey. "I'm going to keep him."

"That's a nice new collar he's wearing," Mother said. "Are you sure he's a stray?"

"I'm sure," Joey told her. Mother stood there for a minute before she went back into the house.

Joey wanted to play some more, but each time he looked at the pup he saw the collar. At last he led the puppy back to the front yard and opened the gate. He put the pup back on the sidewalk. "Go home," he said.

"Hey, that's my dog," a boy about Joey's age shouted. The puppy ran to meet him.

"He's a nice dog," said Joey. "Do you live around here?"

"Yeah. My name's Ricky," he said. "We just moved into that house down the block. Can you come over and play?"

Joey grinned. "Let's go ask my mom."—M.H.D.

Understanding Chases Away Fear

And my father taught me and said. Get wisdom and understanding. Prov. 4:4, 5, ICB.

Timothy and Grandpa began wrestling on the carpet. Timothy quickly wiggled out of Grandpa's hands. Giggling, he rushed around behind Grandpa and threw his arms around Grandpa's neck. Suddenly Timothy stopped laughing, and his eyes grew big and round. He quickly ran as fast as his short brown legs and his blue sneakers could carry him to the far side of the room. He pushed his way up into his daddy's lap and pressed his face against Daddy's shirt.

"What's wrong, Timothy?" Grandpa asked, rushing to him.

Timothy slowly peeked around at Grandpa. "Your head, Grandpa," he said. "What's wrong with your head?"

"My head?" Grandpa asked, looking very surprised. Then Grandpa smiled and laughed. "Oh," he told Daddy, "Timothy has seen the top of my head where there is no hair. My bald spot." Turning to Timothy, Grandpa said, "That's just what happens to some grown-ups when they get older, Timothy. It doesn't hurt me, and it won't hurt you. It feels a lot like your forehead."

Timothy rubbed his fingers across his own forehead.

Then, without speaking, Grandpa leaned down. Timothy carefully patted the brown skin in the middle of Grandpa's black hair. Timothy smiled. The bald spot didn't hurt him or Grandpa.

Sometimes there are things about people that frighten us when we first see them. Their eyes may look much different than ours. Their skin may be a different color, or it may be marked by burns or scars. Their body may be twisted. But when we take time to talk about these things that make people look different, we will begin to understand them. Then we will not be afraid.—F.J.C.

Book Friends

Come, my children, listen to me. Ps. 34:11, NIV.

Shane absolutely hated being sick. He loved to run and jump and play. He loved to roll in the grass and hop and skip and climb. So when he fell from a tree and broke his leg, one of the worst things about it was having to stay in bed. All his friends were in school and could come see him only part of the day. Mom and Dad took turns staying home from work for the first few days, but they too had things they must do. They couldn't stay in his room all the time.

"Mom, what can I do?" he asked over and over.

At last Mom had an idea. "Why don't you visit some good friends you've known for a long time?"

"How?" Shane asked, scowling at his cast.

"Listen, Shane." Mom caught up a pile of books. "Remember how when you read these books you said it was almost like being there with the people in them?" She opened some Easy Readers.

"Yeah, but—"

"Just try it." Mom quietly laid a big Bible picture book Shane hadn't read for a while on top of the others.

All the rest of the time Shane was sick he visited his special "book friends." Best of all were the times when he read his Bible picture book. Good old Daniel, whom God protected by closing the lions' mouths. Noah and his big ark. Jesus, who loved children.

When Shane could go back to school, he promised his book friends he'd come visit them again. "But I hope not with a broken leg," he said.

Do you have any book friends? Which are your favorites?—C.L.R.

Butterfly Boy

You must be patient, my friends, until the Lord comes. James 5:7, REB.

Donald loved the red admiral butterflies that landed on his garage every sunny afternoon just before dinnertime. One day when he and his neighbor Mr. Trich were watching them, Mr. Trich said, "See how the sun shines on the white wall? That's why they come here. They love bright white surfaces."

The next day Donald told his family, "I'll be a bright white surface." He put on his clean dress shirt and stood, still as a statue, in the sun. He did the same thing the next day and the next day and the next.

His sisters laughed at him. His friends said, "Give up, Donald. Those butterflies are never going to land on you."

Donald said, "Yes, they will," and kept going out to stand in the sun.

One day Nancy went outside to call Donald for dinner. Her mouth dropped open, and she rushed to get Ginny and her parents.

Everyone gaped, astonished. Four butterflies were perched on Donald's shirt. Donald's beaming face was brighter than the sun.

After that, Donald's friends and sisters put on bright white shirts and stood outside. Some soon gave up. Others squirmed and moved around. The butterflies landed only on Donald.

"It's not fair," Ginny and Nancy complained to their parents. "What does Donald have that we don't have?"

"Patience," Mother whispered in a voice as soft as a butterfly's touch. —V.L.K.

Do for Others

Do for others what you want them to do for you. Matt. 7:12, TEV.

Eddie frowned. He wished Vic had taken him to the playground. Vic was two years older and lots bigger. And Vic didn't like to play with little kids, even his own brother.

Eddie bounced his basketball against the sidewalk. It was a new ball—a birthday present—but it wasn't much fun playing by himself. He bounced the ball again.

What was that? It looked like someone over there behind the neighbor's hedge. He looked hard at the hedge but he couldn't see anything, so he went back to bouncing his basketball. Dad had even put up a hoop for them, but Vic still wouldn't play with him.

Something moved behind the hedge again. This time Eddie saw a flash of red hair. The new kid next door was watching. Herbie. Herbie was *really* little. Vic wouldn't even *see* a kid that small.

Eddie missed the basketball and swung around to run after it. There stood Herbie, right out in the open, looking at him. Something about Herbie's face reminded Eddie of something.

But he didn't say hi or even let on that he saw Herbie. He just grabbed up his ball and went on bouncing it. The other guys would make fun of him if he hung out with someone that small. They'd ask him if he was baby-sitting, just like Vic said they asked him and—

Eddie stopped bouncing the ball. Now he knew why the look on Herbie's face reminded him of something. He knew that look because he'd seen it when he'd looked in the mirror that morning after Vic said he wouldn't take him along to the playground. Herbie just wanted someone to play with, wanted someone to talk to. Herbie wanted a friend.

Eddie bounced the ball again, carefully keeping his back to the hedge. He had to think about this. He didn't want the fellows to make fun of him, but he did want to have a friend. It looked like Herbie wanted that too.

Eddie took a deep breath and turned around. "Hi, Herbie," he said. "Want to shoot some baskets?"

"Really?" Herbie asked, a big grin coming on his face.

"Really," Eddie said. He grinned too. "Then maybe we can go for a ride on our bikes."—N.C.P.

Overfeeding the Fish

He who covers his sins will not prosper, but whoever confesses and forsakes them will have mercy. Prov. 28:13, NKJV.

"Fish don't need a lot of food," said Joe. "Just a few shakes of this can of fish food will give the fish enough for the whole day."

Joe was feeding his fish while his little brother, Ken, stood watching. Joe had a big fish tank with lots of fish, big ones and small ones of all different colors. He had bought the fish with money earned from doing different jobs. He liked taking care of his fish.

Joe had read books that said that fish don't need much food, so he fed the fish only in the morning. That was enough for the whole day.

When Joe finished feeding the fish, he put the can on the table and left the room. Ken was watching the fish swimming around and coming to the top of the tank to get the food. It was fun to watch their little mouths open and take the tiny pieces of food. After the fish grabbed a bite, they swam back to the bottom of the tank. Pretty soon they swam back to the top to get more food. Soon all the food was gone, but the fish kept coming to the top of the tank looking for more food.

Because the fish kept swimming to the top of the tank, Ken thought the fish were still hungry. *Maybe I'll give them just a little more food*, he thought. He picked up the can and shook it. A few flakes of food came out. "That wasn't very much. I'll shake the can a little harder," Ken said. Ooops! With that last shake, a lot of food spilled into the tank. And the fish hurried to the top of the tank and started eating. Satisfied, Ken put the can beside the tank and left Joe's room.

Later that evening Joe went to his room and saw some of the fish floating on top of the water. They were dead. Ken told his brother that he'd fed the fish more food, thinking they were still hungry. He was sorry that Joe's fish had died, and he asked his brother to forgive him for feeding the fish too much food. Ken took money from his piggy bank and bought more fish for his brother. After that, he was careful not to overfeed the fish.—C.B.T.

Lazybones

Go to the ant, thou sluggard; consider her ways, and be wise. Prov. 6:6, KJV.

"Put your toys away and come help me pull weeds in the garden," Daddy said after breakfast.

Mark didn't want to put his toys away. He didn't want to help. He wanted to feed the ducks. Mark took his toast crust and went outside.

On the way to the pond Mark stopped to look at an ant. Its front half was red and its back half was black. Mark squatted down for a better look. A toast crumb fell on the ground. The ant picked it up and hurried off. Mark followed.

The ant took a tiny little trail in the grass no wider than Mark's finger. It hurried along until it came to a little hill made of pine needles and tiny twigs. There were more red and black ants here.

The ant struggled up the hill with the crumb. It disappeared into one of the holes in the hill. Mark sprinkled more crumbs near the ant path. Then he waited. Soon the ants came. Each one picked up a crumb and carried it away. One ant found a crumb too big to carry. It rushed off and came back with two more ants. Together they picked up the crumb and carried it up the anthill.

Mark was amazed. These ants were hard workers. And they helped each other. Soon the crumbs were all gone.

"I'm a lot bigger than you are," Mark told the ants. "I can work too. I can pull weeds."

Mark sprinkled the rest of the toast crumbs near the anthill. Then he ran to the garden to help Daddy.—M.H.D.

Fuzzy Kitten

Be kind and compassionate to one another. Eph. 4:32, NIV.

Someone dumped Fuzzy, a tiny yellow kitten, on the road. Fuzzy felt scared. And hungry. He cried and cried.

Then Fuzzy saw a house. Maybe he'd find his mother there. He ran to the house.

"Hey, Kenny," Laurie called. "I found a little kitten."

The children fed Fuzzy and played with him. But Fuzzy wanted his mommy. He climbed the steps to the porch and found a huge golden dog sleeping there. Fuzzy knew it wasn't his mother, but the fur looked so soft and warm that he scooted right up to the dog and snuggled against its fur.

But the dog didn't like that. He jumped up and ran away. Fuzzy lay down and meowed.

After a while the dog came back and lay down again. Fuzzy ran and snuggled close to the dog. The dog growled low in his throat and ran away again.

Every time the dog lay down, the kitten ran to snuggle beside it. But the dog jumped up and ran away. Then one day the dog didn't run away, but let the kitten snuggle close. And after that, whenever Fuzzy came up to the dog, the dog lay still and let it cuddle in his fur. Then guess what! One day the dog went looking for the kitten. After that, the dog and cat were best friends.

If someone isn't nice to you, what do *you* do? Do you keep being nice to that person? If you do, that person may turn out to be your best friend. —V.W.

My Poor Roses!

The earth is the Lord's, and everything in it. Ps. 24:1, NIV.

Cathy and her mother lived in a small but comfortable home. They had a chain link fence around their yard, and inside the fence Mother planted a lot of roses. Red roses, yellow ones, pink, white, and even orange. People who passed by stopped to look at the beautiful flowers and smell their sweet scent. Often Cathy's mother cut bouquets and gave them to the neighbors.

Cathy didn't touch the roses, for they had sharp thorns. But she loved their pretty colors and liked to smell them.

Last winter where Cathy lives it got colder than it ever had as long as Mom could remember. Cathy shivered and looked at the rose plants Mother had cut off real short in the fall. Heaps of bark chips protected their roots, but all the stems looked dead.

When spring came, Mother sadly shook her head. She cut the rose stems back until they were only about one inch high, for all the other part was dead. "I don't know if any of them will make it," she told Cathy.

"Couldn't we ask God to make them get well?" Cathy wanted to know.

Mother thought for a little while, then said, "The Bible says the earth and everything in it is the Lord's. I think asking God would be a good idea." So Cathy prayed that God would help the roses grow from the roots that had been deeply buried in the frozen ground.

First one then other bushes had a tiny growth bud. Cathy's mother gave them rose food. Know what? By mid-June, all the roses except one or two had beautiful blossoms, and Cathy was glad.—C.L.R.

The Most Important Ingredient

There are things that last for ever: faith, hope, and love; and the greatest of the three is love. 1 Cor. 13:13, REB.

Torie's kindergarten class was learning about life in the pioneer days. Today they were going to bake corn bread and churn their own butter from cream.

Eric and Taylor measured the dry ingredients for the corn bread while Alex and Olivia measured the wet ingredients. Everyone would have a chance to stir.

When the bowl came around to Torie, she thought of her grandma, who liked to bake. Torie said, "We forgot to put in something important."

Mrs. Falbo looked alarmed. "What?" she asked.

"The love," answered Torie. "My grandma says it's the most important thing."

Mrs. Falbo smiled. "And how does your grandma add the love?"

"Like this," Torie said. "All you have to do is sprinkle it right in. Grandma says that all of us have love right at our fingertips."

Soon the whole class had joined Torie. Everyone was laughing together and sprinkling in love.

When the corn bread was in the oven, it was time to make the butter. Again, everyone would have a chance to churn.

"This is fun," said Noah. "I never knew you made butter this way."

"Let's add love to the butter, too," said Marissa.

The fresh, hand-churned butter on the warm corn bread was a delicious treat for the whole class. And after today they would always remember to add the most important ingredient to everything they made.—V.L.K.

The World Belongs to God

The world and all that is in it belong to the Lord; the earth and all who live on it are his. Ps. 24:1, TEV.

Emily looked at the street outside Grandma's window. Papers were blowing all around, catching on trees, hanging on bushes. It didn't look pretty at all.

Emily remembered how pretty the street had looked last spring, with all the flowers blooming and the trees getting new leaves. Now the street looked bad and dirty.

An old can lay right in the middle of the driveway. Someone had thrown candy wrappers on the ground. They made shiny spots in the flower bed, but they didn't look like flowers. A dirty envelope had blown against the big oak tree in front of the house.

Emily turned from the window. "Grandma," she said, "what's happened to your street? It isn't pretty anymore."

Grandma sighed and looked sad. "I know, child. People are forgetting that God made the world. They're forgetting that it belongs to Him just as we do."

Emily nodded. She knew everyone belonged to God, even the people who didn't know they belonged.

Grandma sighed again. "God made the world, and it still belongs to Him. But He gave it to us to take care of." She started to get up from her chair. "I should put my coat on and go pick up that mess."

"I'll go, Grandma," Emily said. "I can clean it up in a hurry. Then the yard will look all pretty again, like God wants it to look."

Grandma smiled. "That's a good idea. And when you come in, we'll make some cookies. You can take some over to Mrs. Carter later. She's been feeling sad, and maybe some cookies will perk her up."

"Yes, Grandma." Emily smiled. "Grandma?"

"Yes, Emily?"

"God wants us to take care of each other, too, doesn't He?"

Grandma smiled her biggest smile. "That's right, honey."—N.C.P.

Copycat

Don't copy the behavior . . . of this world, but be a new and different person with a fresh newness in all you do and think. Rom. 12:2, TLB.

I have two cats. Puff is my 11-year-old long-haired gray cat with white paws. Charlemagne is my 6-month-old fluffy orange kitten with a cream-colored tip on his tail. Charlemagne would like to be good friends with Puff, but Puff is not interested.

There's probably a good reason Puff doesn't like Charlemagne. Charlemagne will hide on the dining room chair behind the tablecloth. As Puff slowly walks through the dining room, Charlemagne jumps down, right on Puff's back. "Meow!" Puff yowls. Around and around the table they will go. Suddenly Puff stops, hisses a warning, and hits Charlemagne right on his little orange nose.

Charlemagne likes to copy whatever Puff does. If Puff lies on the rug in front of the fire, Charlemagne lies on the rug in front of the fire. If Puff stands by the door meowing to go outside, Charlemagne will suddenly appear so he can go outside too. If Puff lies on the kitchen counter, Charlemagne will be found there too. Charlemagne is a true copycat.

What about you? If the little boy next door uses bad words, will you be extra careful to keep your words pure and kind? If an angry friend sticks out her tongue, will you smile instead? Charlemagne is a cat and doesn't know any better, but you do. When others around you are doing what they should not do, don't be a copycat!—P.M.M.

A Hole in Her Heart

Behold, I come quickly! Hold fast what you have, that no one may take your crown. Rev. 3:11, NKJV.

"Erica, you must not be afraid. The doctors are going to help you to feel better," said Grandmother. "If you promise to do what the doctors tell you, I'll take you to California with me when you're better. How's that?"

Little 6-year-old Erica looked so small lying on her hospital bed. She'd been born with a hole in her heart, and the doctors were trying to help her get better. She'd have to have an operation, they told her. Erica was afraid. She had only her grandmother, since her daddy had died soon after she was born. Erica loved her grandmother, and Grandmother loved Erica.

Grandmother told Erica about California and the pretty places they'd visit once she was better. With tears glistening in her eyes, Erica said she would do what the doctors said. The doctors operated, and Erica did get better.

Several weeks passed. Now they were on their way to California. Grandmother had often told Erica about her father and how she'd see him when Jesus came back to earth. Erica loved to hear about her father and that Jesus was coming back again. As they were driving along, Grandmother said to Erica, "Today is the date that your daddy died."

Erica said happily, "Oh, Grandmother, is Jesus coming today?"

With a puzzled look on her face, Grandmother said, "I don't think so, Erica. Why do you ask?"

Softly Erica said, "Because if Jesus were coming today, I'd see my daddy."

Some day soon Jesus will come again. Do you want Jesus to come again like Erica does?—C.B.T.

Will You Still Love Me?

Let not your heart be troubled, neither let it be afraid. John 14:27, KJV.

Josie followed her mother around the kitchen while she got dinner ready. It was going to happen soon. Mommy had said so. Josie wondered if what Susan had told her was true.

"Mommy, would you still love me if I tracked mud all over the rug?"

"Uh huh," her mother said, slicing up vegetables for the salad.

Josie could tell Mommy wasn't really listening. "Would you still love me if I wrote on the walls with my color crayons?"

"Stop being silly and go play," her mother told her.

Josie didn't want to go play. She had to know. "Would you still love me if I said bad words?" She followed her mother into the dining room. "Would Daddy still love me if I pulled up his flowers or hit the dog with a big stick?"

Mother eased herself down into a chair by the table and took Josie's hand. "Daddy and I wouldn't like it if you did all those things. But we would still love you."

Josie reached out and put a hand on Mommy's tummy. "Will you still love me when the new baby comes?" she asked in a very small voice. "Susan says that you and Daddy won't."

"Oh, Josie, is that what this is all about?" Mother put her arms around Josie and held her close. "Of course we will. You're our little girl, and we'll always love you. Nothing will ever change that. Not even the new baby."

Josie breathed a big sigh and hugged her mother. "Can I go watch TV until Daddy comes home?" she asked.—M.H.D.

God Knows All About You

You saw my bones being formed as I took shape in my mother's body. When I was put together there, you saw my body as it was formed. All the days planned for me were written in your book before I was one day old. Ps. 139:15, 16, ICB.

Jimmika (jim-ME-ka) slowly turned around so that Auntie Mae and Grandfather could see the shiny, pink satin bow at the back of her new dress.

"It's beautiful!" Auntie Mae said. Then facing Mother, she asked, "And you bought this size 2 dress before Jimmika was born?"

"Yes," Mother answered. "Dr. Smith showed me the ultrasound* pictures he'd taken of Jimmika. It was so exciting. Ultrasound lets doctors see babies before they're born so they can make sure everything is all right. As soon as Dr. Smith told me I was going to have a little girl, I rushed to the store and bought this dress. I had seen it the week before."

Jimmika smiled. She liked to hear the story of her picture being made before she was born.

"Doctors are able to do wonderful things these days," Auntie Mae said, closing a pink barrette on Jimmika's braid.

"If you think that's wonderful, you should read what God can do," Grandfather told them. He held his Bible up in the air for them to see. Then he turned to our Scripture text and read it out loud. "God knows Jimmika better than any of us does—even Doctor Smith," Grandfather added.

"And my Sabbath school teacher says that God loves me more than anyone else," Jimmika said.

"That's why He makes sure that He knows all about you," Grandpa told her. "And that's how we can know how much we love Him."

You can learn more about God every time someone reads your Sabbath school lesson to you. Be sure to listen carefully so you can get to know God better each day.—F.J.C.

---

* made with sound waves, at the hospital

The Best Present Ever

Good will come to him that is generous and lends freely. Ps. 112:5, NIV.

Mary listened hard to the minister when he said, "The best present ever is the one you give when it's needed most. God gave His Son so that all people might live. He wants us to give things to others, too."

All week Mary remembered what Pastor Graham said. But she was just a little girl. How could she give what he called "the best present ever"?

Mary was glad when Friday came. Her friend Cammy was going to spend the weekend with her grandma, who lived next door to Mary. The girls would go to church together.

Cammy lived several miles away, so she brought a pretty dress and her good sandals. Friday afternoon the girls played in the yard. So did Cub, a big, friendly dog. Then all of a sudden he grabbed one of Cammy's sandals and raced off! All the girls' calling didn't bring him back. When he finally came home several hours later, he didn't have the sandal with him. Cammy's sandal was gone.

"I can't go to church with just one shoe!" Cammy cried.

"The dog ate her shoe. I mean, he stole it," Mary told Cammy's grandma.

"Oh dear." Grandma looked troubled.

"Wait!" Mary ran home, grabbed her own sandals, and raced back. "Look, Cammy. I can wear my tennis shoes to church. God won't care."

"I think God will be very pleased," Grandma said when Cammy put on the sandals. Mary felt so happy about sharing that she didn't mind wearing her old tennis shoes at all. —C.L.R.

Condensed from *Primary Treasure*, Apr. 2, 1988.

The Glistening Spider Web

Blessed are the gentle; they shall have the earth for their possession. Matt. 5:5, REB.

Joshua and Jeremy were outside playing when Chris came over. "Let's play on the tire swing," Chris said.

"OK."

Suddenly Jeremy stopped. "Wow, look at this!" he said. The boys gathered around him and looked where he pointed. They saw a huge spider web stretching between two yew bushes near the patio. On this early morning the spider web was still covered with glistening drops of dew.

"Watch this," Chris said suddenly. He picked up a stick and wrecked the spider web with it.

The confused, dizzy spider swung by a long strand of silk, then raced up a branch.

Chris pulled out the stick. "It's all sticky from the spider web. How neat."

"I don't think it's neat," said Joshua. "Why did you wreck the spider web? It was beautiful."

Jeremy added, "Now the poor spider has to build another one, and that takes a long time. How'd you like it if some giant came and wrecked *your* house in a second?"

Chris hung his head. "I'd hate it," he said. "I'm sorry. I never thought about it like that."

The next day Chris came over again. When he walked past the yew bushes, he thought sadly about yesterday's mistake. Then he noticed a new spider web. It seemed to be bigger and more sparkling than before.

"Let's go," said Joshua and Jeremy, racing toward the tire swing.

"Just a minute," Chris said.

He stared at the glistening spider web. Then he smiled and dashed off to join his friends.—V.L.K.

Show Respect

Show respect for old people and honor them. Lev. 19:32, TEV.

"But Mother," Molly said, "I want to play with Susan."

"Later, Molly. Mrs. Adams is waiting for you."

Molly sighed. "But Mrs. Adams is so old. And she tells the same stories over and over."

Mother smiled. "And that's why she needs your help."

Molly put on her coat.

"When you finish, be sure to ask her if there's anything else you can do."

"Yes, Mother."

Molly went through the hole in the hedge and up to Mrs. Adams' back door. As soon as she was in the house she began hurrying through the chores. She took out the garbage. She swept the floors. *If I'm really fast*, she thought, *maybe I can still play with Susan.*

At last she was finished. She put the broom away, then remembered what Mother had told her. "Mrs. Adams, is there anything else I can do for you today?"

"Well, dear, the furniture does need dusting. It's so hard for me to reach."

"That's all right," Molly said with a sigh. "I'll do it." She knew that by the time she finished, Susan would have to go in for supper. Molly dusted all the furniture. Then she went out to the kitchen. "I'm all done," she said.

Mrs. Adams nodded. "One more thing, dear."

Molly sighed. "Yes, Mrs. Adams?"

"I could use some help baking some brownies."

"Brownies?" Molly smiled. "Brownies are my most favorite cookies."

Mrs. Adams grinned. "I know. Mine, too."

When Molly went home to supper, she took a plate of brownies. "We made cookies," she told Mother, "and Mrs. Adams told me the best stories about when she was a little girl."—N.C.P.

In the Hospital

Let him have all your worries and cares, for he is always thinking about you and watching everything that concerns you. 1 Peter 5:7, TLB.

Early in the morning Mama and Daddy walked with 3-year-old Ryan into the hospital. This was the day Ryan would have surgery on his ears and have his tonsils and adenoids removed. The doctor told Ryan the surgery would help his ears feel much better than they had felt for the past few months.

Mom and Dad quietly wondered, "Will he be terribly afraid? Will he cry or fuss when he has to go with the nurses and doctors?" But they knew that Grandma and Grandpa were praying for Ryan. Aunt Lori and Uncle Todd were praying, and many friends were praying, too.

While Ryan, Mama, and Daddy waited in the admissions area, Daddy suggested they pray. "Dear Jesus," Daddy said softly, "we ask you especially to be with Ryan today. Be with the doctors and help Ryan to know that his angel will be right there with him. Thank You, Father. Amen."

Before long a doctor walked up holding a teddy bear. "He will go in the operating room too," the doctor explained to Ryan. Ryan liked that idea.

The surgery went well. The nurses told Mama and Daddy that Ryan had been a wonderful patient.

Later Mama said to Ryan, "Tell me about the operating room." Ryan thought for a moment and then said, "Well, a man put a mask on my bear, and then he put a mask on me."

"Were you afraid?" Mama asked.

"No," Ryan said. "I just went to sleep."

Mama knew God had been with Ryan. If you ask God, He will always be with you, too.

Can you remember some times when God was with you?—P.M.M.

Fingerprint Jello

And be sure your sin will find you out. Num. 32:23, NKJV.

"There, the jello is all made," said Grandmother. "Now I will put it in the refrigerator, and when it gets hard we will eat it for supper."

Five-year-old Maryanne loved jello. She could hardly wait until suppertime. She tried to play with her dolls, but all she could think about was the pretty, green jello sitting in the refrigerator.

"Grandma," called Maryanne, "is the jello ready yet?"

"I don't think so, but it will be soon," said Grandmother.

Maryanne went outside to ride on her tricycle. She rode for a little while, but her mind was on the jello in the refrigerator.

I wonder if it's ready? thought Maryanne. *I'll just go and look. Grandma will never know.* She got off her tricycle and went inside the house to the kitchen. Grandmother was in living room talking with Mrs. Smith, her neighbor, and she didn't hear her come in. Maryanne opened the refrigerator door and there on the shelf sat the big bowl of green jello.

Looking at the jello and wondering if it was ready to eat, Maryanne put her finger right on its shining green top. To her surprise, it felt hard. So she walked her fingers right across its surface. Ooooo, it felt cool and nice.

After dinner Grandmother went to the refrigerator and brought out the jello. As she was carrying it to the table, she asked a funny question. "What little girl took a walk through my jello?" she asked.

Maryanne looked surprised. "It was me, Grandma."

Grandmother put the dish on the table and there all over the jello were Maryanne's fingerprints.

Tears came into Maryanne's eyes. "I'm sorry," she said. "I didn't mean to make the jello ugly. It felt nice, and I didn't think it would hurt anything. Please forgive me."

"I forgive you, child." Then Grandmother pulled her chair close to Maryanne's and gave her a little hug. "I may not have seen you touch the jello, but Jesus saw you. So let's ask Jesus to forgive you too." Grandmother and Maryanne knelt together and prayed. Maryanne felt a lot better after that.

Can you think of a time when you were naughty and asked Jesus to forgive you?—C.B.T.

The Snake Gift— A Mission Story

Oh that men would praise the Lord for his goodness, and for his wonderful works to the children of men! Ps. 107:31, KJV.

It was early evening, and we had just come home from the Friday night meeting at the church. "Come quickly," someone called. "There's a big snake caught on the fence!"

We ran to the back fence of the place where we lived in Singapore. There we saw a beautiful large snake with dark-brown spots on its bright-yellow skin. It looked bigger around than your daddy's leg and much, much longer.

"It's a python," someone said. "Be real careful! It can wrap itself around animals and squeeze so tight that it kills them."

We all stood around to see what would happen. It looked as though the python had just eaten a neighbor's chicken. He had swallowed it whole and then tried to climb over the fence. But the poor chicken had made a big lump in his long body and that lump was caught on the fence. The python was stuck.

Because pythons are dangerous and no one wanted it, we had to decide what to do with it. No one wanted to kill it. So eight men used all their strength to free it off the fence and put it into a great big box. What beautiful, tough skin it had!

Now, what would you do with a 15-foot python if it came into your backyard? We missionaries stood beside the box and talked. We had prayed for money to tell others about Jesus. Could God have sent this python as an answer to our prayers? A few days later we sold it to a pet shop. We thanked God for sending this special gift, a python, so we could give an offering to Jesus.

Do you remember to praise God for the nice things He gives you? What are you especially thankful for right now?—E.E.L.

A Happy Feeling

For where your treasure is, there your heart will be also. Matt. 6:21, NIV.

Sally hurried to keep up with her older sister Carrie and Carrie's friend Jana. As they passed the playground, they saw two ladies sitting at a small table. Beside them were four or five wire cages with people crowded around them.

"What are they doing?" Sally asked.

"The sign by the table says 'Free dogs to a good home,' " said Carrie.

"Let's go see them," said Jana, and they hurried inside the fence.

Sally had never seen so many dogs in one place before. Big ones and little ones. Some looked scared and some looked sad.

"The old lady who owns the dogs got sick and had to go to the hospital," the boy beside Sally explained. "When she got well enough to tell somebody about the dogs, they were half starved and some of them were sick. Those ladies are taking donations to pay for their food and medicine until they find homes for the dogs."

Sally looked at the dogs again. Then she walked over to the table. She opened her little purse. "This is all the money I have," she said, emptying the coins out onto the table. "I want to help the dogs."

The lady looked surprised. "Are you sure you want to donate all your money?" she said. Sally nodded.

"That was a dumb thing to do," said Jana when they left the playground and started down the street again. "Now you don't have anything."

Sally stopped for a second, then smiled. "Yes, I do. I have a happy feeling all over."

She spread her arms like wings and ran all the way to the corner. —M.H.D.

Follow the Leader

He said . . . , Follow me. Luke 9:59, KJV.

Three-year-old Judi loved her big sister, Jill, a lot. Jill knew everything. When Judi put on her shoes, Jill hurried to tie them for her. When Judi needed someone to push a button through the buttonhole, Jill always fixed it for her. Jill could draw pictures of trees and rivers. Judi didn't know how. Jill was so big and smart. Judi thought that no one had ever had such a nice big sister before.

One day Daddy, Mommy, Jill, and Judi went out to a restaurant for dinner.

When the waiter brought big bowls of salad, Judi saw long white strips of something she didn't recognize. "What's this?" she asked.

"That's lettuce," Mommy said. "We have it at home, but ours is green and we don't cut it into such skinny strips."

Judi still wasn't sure about it. She turned to her big sister. "Jill," she said, "do we like lettuce?"

Mommy gave Jill a quick look and nodded her head up and down. Jill shoved a bite into her mouth. "Yes," she said. "We love lettuce."

It's fine for little sisters to follow big sisters, but we must be careful to follow only people who are doing good things. Do you know who's the very best one to follow? That's right. Jesus. He's our perfect leader.

Do you have older friends or relatives who help you know what to do? —V.W.

Buddies at Last

How good and pleasant it is when brothers live together in unity! Ps. 133:1, NIV.

Sugar, the big black Labrador retriever, and Smokey, the gray-striped cat, lived a happy life with their family. Dad, Mom, Julie, Kelly, and David loved the animals. They took good care of them.

"Why don't Sugar and Smokey play together?" the children sometimes wanted to know.

"Dogs and cats aren't always good friends," Dad told them. "They get along, but they aren't really buddies."

All spring and summer and fall Sugar and Smokey chased the children on the green lawn, rolled in the falling leaves when they came down—and ignored each other. Then winter came—one of the coldest winters their town had ever seen. Down, down, down went the little red line in the big outdoor thermometer. "Brrr, brrr, brrr," said the family.

Sugar and Smokey's fur grew thick to keep them warm, but the weather got colder and colder. One morning the family discovered that the big Lab and the gray-striped cat had become buddies at last. Both lay inside Sugar's warm doghouse, fighting the cold by being close together. For the rest of the winter Smokey and Sugar slept together, and not until it got warmer did Smokey go back to his own warm house.

God wants us to get along and be buddies with our brothers and sisters, too. And not just in cold weather!—C.L.R.

Good Shepherds

If one of you has a hundred sheep and loses one of them, does he not leave the ninety-nine in the wilderness and go after the one that is missing until he finds it? Luke 15:4, REB.

"It's not fair," Mark complained about his nursery school teacher, "the way Mrs. Edson treats us."

Mama frowned. "You've always thought that she was a wonderful teacher. What has she done that isn't fair?"

"There's a new boy in our class named Adams," Mark explained. "He moved here because his parents got divorced. At least that's what Jackie told me. And he acts up all the time. But instead of punishing him, Mrs. Edson just stops what she's doing—even if the rest of us are having fun—and sits him on her lap. It's not fair!" Mark stomped his foot.

Mama smiled. "Seems to me that it's the right thing to do."

Mark frowned, and Mama continued. "Do you remember the story in the Bible about the good shepherd who left 99 sheep behind to find the one that was lost?"

"Well, Adam is like that little lost sheep, Mark. He must feel lonely and sad and confused. Mrs. Edson is acting like the good shepherd. She loves all of you, but she knows which one needs extra care and attention right now. That's why she goes to him."

"H'mmm," Mark said.

Mama added, "And I'll bet you could be be a good shepherd too, and help Adam feel like he really belongs in the class."

Mark laughed. "You mean in the flock?"

"Exactly," she said, hugging him. Then she laughed too.—V.L.K.

Praise the Lord

Praise the Lord's glorious name. 1 Chron. 16:29, TEV.

Dottie looked at last year's Easter dress. "Mother, I need a new dress. This one's too small."

Mother looked up from the patch she was sewing on brother Buster's jeans. "I'm sorry, Dottie, but I don't think we can get you a new dress this year."

"But it's for Easter!" Dottie cried. "All the girls are getting new dresses. I can't wear this old thing."

Mother took another stitch. "You don't have to wear that dress, Dottie. But there's just no way we can buy you a new one." She smiled. "I could put a ruffle around the bottom. And some little flowers on the collar. That will make it look different."

"It'll still be the same old dress," Dottie said.

Mother looked sad. "Dottie, you've got the wrong idea. We don't go to church to show off our clothes. We go to praise the Lord."

Tears ran down Dottie's cheeks. "I don't care. I want a new dress." She was still crying when she ran out of the house. *It's just not fair*, she thought, crawling into her hiding place under the grapevine. *Other kids get new clothes. Why can't I?* After a while a little grape leaf started to tickle her neck. Dottie pulled it off and looked at it. In the summer the grapes would smell so good. They'd taste good, too. It was nice of God to make the grapes.

Then she thought how God had made Mother and Daddy, and Buster, and given them a house to live in, and the grapevine hiding place, and—

Dottie wiped away her tears and crawled out of her hiding place. She ran into the house and found Mother. "Mother," she said, "I want to go to church on Easter and praise God. Will you fix my dress for me?"

Mother gave her a big hug. "Of course, Dottie. We'll praise the Lord together."—N.C.P.

The Penguin Surprise

Watch for the new thing I am going to do. Isa. 43:19, TEV.

"I want to see the lions and tigers and elephants," Gene all but shouted from the back seat of the car.

"I want to see the bears!" Jim said.

The family had left early in the morning for a special trip to the big city. The boys were excited about all the different animals they'd see at the zoo. First the family made its way to the big cats—the lions and tigers. But as they started up the sidewalk, Dad noticed a sign. "This area temporarily closed," he read aloud.

"Oh, no," Gene cried.

"Well, let's go see the bears," Jim told him. But the bears were all asleep or in their dens. They weren't any fun at all. Next the family walked through a cage so big that it was like several rooms put together. It was filled with tall plants and lots of different birds were flying around it. That was interesting. But at the entrance of the elephant area they saw another sign: "Will reopen in the spring." How disappointing!

It was almost too much when the family saw the "Closed" sign at the petting zoo. But they kept on walking. "Let's see what's in this building," Dad suggested.

A real surprise awaited the family in the cool penguin house. Through the glass walls the boys watched tall penguins waddling on icy slopes. They saw penguins with crests of feathers on their heads, and penguins with bright orange patches on their heads. The most fun was watching the penguins line up to take turns jumping in a pool of water, then pop back up, landing on the bank. The boys laughed and laughed.

What had been quite a disappointing day had turned into a wonderful and fun time. Everyone laughed again when they heard little Jim making up his own words to the song "Lift Up the Trumpet": "Cheer up, ye penguins, be joyful and sing . . ."

Next time you feel disappointed, cheer up. There may be something better than you expected waiting for you.—P.M.M.

Mangoes on the Tree of Life?—A Mission Story

Oh, taste and see that the Lord is good; blessed is the man who trusts in Him! Ps. 34:8, NKJV.

Have you ever eaten a mango? Have you ever even *seen* a mango? Do you know what a mango is?

A mango is a pear-shaped fruit with a big seed inside it. The seed is almost as big as the mango itself. Mangoes grow on tall trees where there's lots of hot sunshine. The skin of the mango is green, but when it's ready to eat, the skin is a nice yellow, and a little soft when you press it. Oh, it tastes so good and sweet!

The best-tasting and sweetest mangoes are those that stay on the tree until they are ripe—ready to eat. They are sweet and juicy. When our family lived in Brazil, we had two mango trees in our backyard. My children would go out and look at the mangoes to see if there were any ripe ones to eat. Finally a lot of the mangoes started to turn yellow. Day after day the children looked up at the mangoes to see if they could find a ripe one. One day they knocked a green mango off the tree, but it didn't taste very good.

At last the mangoes were ripe. Some fell off the tree when the wind blew hard, and some were knocked off the tree when it rained. But the children scrambled up the trunk of the mango tree and picked most of them for us to eat. Now that I live in the United States, I miss eating good, sweet mangoes. Of course, I can find them at the store now and then, but they're not sweet like the ones we had in Brazil. Sometimes I say, "I hope Jesus has a mango tree for me in heaven."

Jesus will have a tree in heaven covered with good, juicy, sweet fruit for us to eat. That tree is called the tree of life, and it will have 12 different kinds of fruit on it. Someday soon we'll be with Jesus and we'll eat that wonderful sweet fruit. I can hardly wait.

(NOTE TO READERS: You can read about the tree of life in Rev. 22:1. If mangoes are in season, it would be fun to go to the grocery and find a mango to eat.)—C.B.T.

The Friendly Side of Dark

You will not fear the terror of the night. Ps. 91:5, RSV.

Daddy gave Danny a piggyback ride up to bed. He tucked him in and gave him a kiss. "Good night," Daddy said.

Danny sat up when Daddy started to turn off the light. "Leave it on," he said.

"You can't sleep with the light on," said Daddy.

"Then leave the door open. Please," Danny begged.

"Is something wrong?" Daddy asked, sitting down on his bed.

Danny's voice sounded small and shaky. "I'm scared of the dark," he said.

"There's no reason to be afraid of the dark," Daddy told him. "It's not being able to see in the dark that makes you afraid."

"Then I wish it would stay daylight all the time," said Danny.

Daddy smiled. "I don't think that would be such a great idea. God made the night so His creatures can rest."

"What creatures?" Danny raised up on one elbow and looked around. He hoped none of the creatures were hiding in his closet or under the bed.

"The birds and the insects and the animals are some of God's creatures," Daddy answered. "When the sun goes down, they know night is coming, and they hurry back to their homes. And when darkness comes, they sleep and rest."

"Oh, I never thought about that," said Danny. "Am I one of God's creatures too?"

"We all are," said Daddy.

"And when darkness comes, is that when God turns out His lights so all His creatures can sleep?" Danny asked.

Daddy chuckled. "I guess you could say that."

"Then I'm not afraid anymore." Danny snuggled down under the covers. "You can turn out the light." He was almost asleep when Daddy closed the door.—M.H.D.

Helping Friends

Be kind and loving to each other. Eph. 4:32, ICB.

Ty was the only 6-year-old boy at the family reunion held in the amusement park. His sister and his girl cousins never wanted to go on the rides he chose. He soon grew tired of tagging along with them.

Kicking up stones and dust with the toe of his white sneaker, Ty walked slowly toward the picnic shelter. Then he spied Muzzie's bright-yellow blouse. Walking faster, he thought about how he and Muzzie, his grandmother, had often gone roller skating and bicycle riding and played catch!

Soon Muzzie held Ty's hand as they walked toward the merry-go-round. After that, they rode the train around the park.

"What's next?" Muzzie asked.

"Let's ride the ski lift!" Ty squealed.

"Well . . . it looks like I can almost reach up and touch the seats," Muzzie said thoughtfully as a string of riders passed overhead.

When it came to high rides, Muzzie always said, "Not me!"

"This is going to be fun!" Ty reassured Muzzie as the attendant snapped their seat railing shut.

Quickly the ski lift rose until they were looking down at the treetops.

"I'm scared!" Muzzie gasped. Ty had never seen that expression on her face before.

"Muzzie, you know God wouldn't let us fall," Ty said softly, taking her hand. Muzzie almost smiled.

Finally they were walking down the ramp to ground level.

"Let's try the bumper cars!" Muzzie said. Ty was glad to see her wearing a real smile again. And she kissed his nose.

Grown-ups are afraid of some things. When you find out about those things, do you laugh and make fun of the grown-ups? Or do you remind them of Jesus' protection?

(NOTE TO READERS: Think back and tell your child some things you were afraid of when you were his or her age. Let your child talk about his or her fears, then talk about God's care.)—F.J.C.

Too High for Tammy

Is not God in the heights of heaven? Job 22:12, NIV.

Tammy had a terrible problem. She wanted to go with her grandmother to visit some cousins in another state. But every time she saw a big airplane like the one they had to fly in to get there, she got scared.

Maybe it happened because a long time ago, so long she could just barely remember, she fell down a long flight of stairs. All she could think about was the empty space beneath her. Yet how could she tell Grandma? Would Grandma laugh, the way Tammy's brother did when she told him she didn't want to go in an airplane?

Seven days, then six, then five, and at last there were only four days until it was time to go. Tammy waited until her teasing brother had gone outside, then she slipped into Grandma's lap. "I—I—don't want to go," she whispered.

Grandma looked surprised. "I thought you really wanted to see your cousins."

"I do." Hot tears stung Tammy's eyes, and she hugged her grandmother. "But I don't want to go on an airplane."

"A lot of people are afraid to fly," Grandma said. "I used to be frightened myself."

Tammy felt surprised. Grandma often flew to come see them.

"Tammy," Grandma told her, "listen to this." She opened her Bible and read the verse we just read to begin this story. "God is everywhere, and we don't have to be afraid."

Guess what? Tammy felt a whole lot better.—C.L.R.

The Smallest Sunflower

I have come that they may have life, and that they may have it more abundantly. John 10:10, NKJV.

Three sunflowers grew together. One three-foot sunflower looked up at the six-foot giants on either side of it.

It tried stretching and craning its green stem-neck. Still, it could not match the height of its huge companions.

Finally the other sunflowers lifted their golden faces to the sun. The smallest sunflower stood in their shadows and bowed its tiny head.

Fall came. The striped seeds on the sunflowers grew ripe. Cardinals, juncos, and blue jays plucked them from the giants' heavy heads. A tiny chickadee tried, but the other birds pecked her away.

The bigger birds ate every seed on the giants. Then they noticed the smallest sunflower. They tried to perch on it, but it couldn't hold them. Their weight bent it to the ground.

The chickadee saw her chance. She perched lightly atop the smallest sunflower. It held her like a hammock. One by one, she plucked a seed and flitted to a nearby tree to enjoy it.

On one trip to her tree, the chickadee dropped a seed. It sank into the soft, wet earth for a long winter's nap. In the spring the chickadee built her nest. One day she noticed a new three-foot-tall plant growing near her tree.

In the summer the new plant lifted its golden face to the sun. Its striped seeds grew ripe in the fall and fed the chickadee and her new family well.

On one trip back to the tree, one of the young chickadees dropped a seed. It sank into the soft, wet earth . . .

(NOTE TO READERS: Go to the store and buy a bag of sunflower seeds for the birds. Or buy a small bag of sunflower seeds for you and your child to share. Draw a picture of a sunflower and glue the striped seeds in its center.)—V.L.K.

New Being

When anyone is joined to Christ, he is a new being; the old is gone, the new has come. 2 Cor. 5:17, TEV.

Jill sighed. The table had to be set for supper. Then she had to dust the living room. She didn't mind setting the table, but she didn't like to dust. Dust tickled her nose and made her sneeze. And the next day everything had to be dusted again.

She went to the cupboard and took out the dishes. Mother looked up from peeling potatoes at the sink. "Your setting the table is such a big help to me."

"I like to help," Jill said with a smile.

"What Bible verse did you learn in Sabbath school this week?" Mother asked.

Jill thought a moment. "I can't remember all the words, but it was something about being a new person."

Mother nodded. "That's probably the verse about being joined to Christ."

"That's it," Jill said. "But I don't feel new. I feel like the same old me—the one who doesn't like to dust." She sighed. "I don't think I'll ever *like* to dust."

Mother chuckled. "I don't think the verse means that we'll *like* everything we have to do. But a person who believes in Jesus wants to do God's will."

Jill thought about that. "I think I see." She put the last plate on the table. "Being a new me means doing what's right, even if I don't like it."

"That's it," Mother said.

Jill gave Mother a hug. "Well, I don't know if it's the new me or the old me, but I'm going to go and dust the living room."

Mother smiled and hugged her back. "I think it's the new you."—N.C.P.

The Borrowed Snorkel— A Mission Story

What shall I do? . . . It was . . . borrowed. 2 Kings 6:5, TEV.

"Come on, everyone. Let's go out to the coral reef!" shouted 6-year-old Russell.

Russell and his missionary family were on a much-needed vacation. They had rented a small block cabin on the Indian Ocean in the country of Kenya. Friends had lent them snorkeling equipment so they could explore the nearby coral reef.

With snorkels and masks everyone enjoyed viewing the beautiful underwater sights—big fish, little fish, coral in the shape of bushes, coral that looked dainty and lacy, coral in colors of soft yellow, rose, purple, and tan.

Dad was the first to notice the tide coming in. "Hey, let's hurry back to the beach," he called. "The tide's coming in!"

Russell's younger sister Becky obeyed, splashing toward the beach. But Russell stayed in the shallow water and put on his mask and snorkel to check out the sandy bottom. He put his face in the foamy water hoping to see something interesting. Russell never even saw the wave that sent him tumbling.

"Oh, no," cried Russell, wiping the salty water from his eyes, "my snorkel is gone!" Mom looked. Dad looked. Becky looked. There was no snorkel to be found.

That evening at worship the family knelt together, and Dad prayed, "Dear Lord, You know how bad we feel about our friend's lost snorkel. If it is Your will, help us find it."

After prayer the family decided to take a night walk along the beach. With the waves splashing at his side, Russell ran ahead playing in the flashlight beam. Suddenly he stopped. There at his feet in a pile of seaweed was the lost snorkel. The family again knelt for prayer—this time to say thank You.

(NOTE TO READERS: Look on a map or globe and find the country of Kenya and the Indian Ocean.)—P.M.M.

Only an Onion

For I was hungry and you gave Me food; I was thirsty and you gave Me drink; I was a stranger and you took Me in. Matt. 25:35, NKJV.

An onion for breakfast? or lunch? or dinner? How would you like that? It's not a very good meal, is it? But when that's all you have to eat . . .

A man stood looking in a garbage can. Before long he pulled something out—an onion. Then he sat down on the ground and began to eat it.

How could he eat an old dirty onion, and all by itself, you might want to know. The man could do it because he was hungry.

Do you think Jesus was sad seeing that man going into a garbage can to find something to eat? It's sad to know that even in a country where there is plenty of food, many boys and girls and mothers and fathers go to bed hungry every night.

Jesus has promised something wonderful for those who love and obey Him. When we get to heaven, Jesus will have a great supper waiting for us. He calls it a "banquet." Great big, long tables will be covered with good things to eat. Your favorite fruits will be there. Maybe we'll have some of that fruit from the Garden of Eden.

It makes Jesus happy to plan a wonderful banquet for us. And it makes Jesus happy when we are kind to others. If you ever have a chance to share your food with someone who doesn't have any, do what Jesus would do—share yours. When you're kind and helpful to others, it's just as if you're doing it to Jesus.

Pray for boys and girls who may not have as much food as you have, and pray that you will be willing to share what you have with those who may be in need.—C.B.T.

The Little Yellow Bulldozer

The eyes of the Lord are in every place, beholding the evil and the good. Prov. 15:3, KJV.

The sandbox was empty when Juan came out to play after lunch. He looked around the courtyard hoping to see his friends. But he was alone.

"I'll build a big hill and a road over it and around it," Juan told himself. "Soon Zack and Aaron will come out to help me."

Juan put down his pail and started to dig with his shovel. He filled the pail over and over again and dumped it in the middle of the sandbox. The hill grew higher and higher.

Suddenly Juan's shovel struck something hard. He dug away the sand. There was Zack's little yellow bulldozer. It had been lost for a long time. Juan ran his hand over the shiny yellow paint.

"If this bulldozer was mine I could build lots of good roads," Juan said. He looked around the courtyard again. He was still alone. Juan put the bulldozer on the sidewalk. He guided it around in a circle. Still no one came. Slowly Juan pushed the bulldozer into the shadows of the slide. He peeked to see if anyone was looking. Then Juan hid the bulldozer under his jacket and hurried to the apartment across the courtyard. When he knocked on a door, Zack answered.

"Come play in the sand with me," said Juan.

"I don't want to," said Zack, looking sad. "Somebody stole my new bulldozer."

"It wasn't stolen." With a big smile on his face, Juan opened his jacket.

"My bulldozer!" Zack shouted. "Where did you find it?"

"Buried in the sand," Juan answered.

"Now we can make lots of roads and streets." Zack grinned. "And you get to use the bulldozer first. Come on, I'll race you back to the sandbox."—M.H.D.

The Big Fall

Those who think themselves great shall be disappointed and humbled. Matt. 23:12, TLB.

"Mommy, come see our parade," Janie called.

Mommy hurried out to watch the kids ride around several trees in the backyard. Janie, 5, rode a big tricycle. Cindy, 3, rode a small tricycle. Tiny Nan, 1½ years old, rode a little "powder puff" cycle.

They rode around the loop awhile. But Janie got bored. She stopped her tricycle where Mommy could watch her. Then she climbed up and stood on the seat with one foot. She curved her other foot out in front of her and circled her arms daintily over her head. "Look, Mommy," she called. "I'm a beautiful ballerina. The greatest and most beautiful ballerina in the world."

Suddenly Mommy yelled, "Janie, get down! Hurry! Jump down, quick!"

Then Janie heard a big bang and the seat she stood on started jiggling. She tried to stay up, but she fell down hard. Baby Nan had run into her tricycle. Janie fell on the front of Nan's powder puff. It hurt her mouth and she started crying.

Mommy cuddled Janie close and wiped away the blood. "I know it hurts, love," she said. "But it'll feel better in a minute."

"The Bible tells us that if we think we're great, we'll be disappointed." She hugged Janie closer. "But you *were* a beautiful ballerina!"—V.L.W.

Special Cookout

I lift up my eyes to the hills—where does my help come from? My help comes from the Lord, the Maker of heaven and earth. Ps. 121:1, 2, NIV.

Joel could hardly wait for Dad to get home. The minute the crew bus stopped in front of their country home and Dad stepped down, he ran out to give him a hug. Joel helped Dad carry his lunch bucket. Dad carried his tools, too, for he worked in the woods and liked his own equipment.

"You aren't too tired, are you, Dad?" Joel anxiously asked.

"No way." Dad's eyes twinkled just like Joel's. "All day at work I've been thinking about our special cookout."

"I'm glad we live where we can walk over a field and down a hill to the river," Joel said.

"So am I." Dad grinned. "Are we all ready to go?"

"Oh, yes. Mom's wrapping up baby Charlie and I helped her put potatoes and corn in a sack. Yummm. They're so good roasted in a fire. And there's tomatoes and apple cake, and—"

"Whoa! You'll get me so hungry I can't wait," Dad teased.

Down by the river Dad made their campfire. Joel waded in a little creek but stayed back from where it ran into the big river. While they ate he looked up at the beautiful, snow-covered Mount White Horse. "Dad, does God live on top of the mountain?" he asked.

"God is everywhere, son. Your mother and I feel that God must love mountains, for He made many beautiful ones."

"I love mountains too," Joel said. "And God."

Do you love mountains? Most important, do you love God? He loves you—a lot.

(NOTE TO READERS: Talk about other beautiful things God has made.)—C.L.R.

Life, Little or Large

The wolf and the lamb will feed together and the lion will eat straw like the ox. . . . Neither hurt nor harm will be done in all my holy mountain, says the Lord. Isa. 65:25, REB.

Over and over again Patrick slapped his shovel on the sidewalk.

"What are you doing?" Grandma asked.

"Smashing ants," Patrick answered. He slapped another one.

"Why?" Grandma asked.

Patrick shrugged. "I don't know."

"Insects are living things," Grandma explained. "They have a place in the world, just like everything else that was created. Do you think it's right to destroy God's creation?"

"No," Patrick said softly. He thought for a moment. "Grandma, did God make mice?"

"Yes, Patrick. God made every creature. He is the giver of all life."

"Then why doesn't God mind when Fluffy catches mice?" Patrick asked.

"God put people, His highest creatures, in charge of all the others," Grandma explained. "After sin came into the world, the animals began fighting. Many different animals depend on catching other animals for food."

"Fluffy doesn't need to catch mice," Patrick said. "We give her lots of cat food."

Grandma laughed. "You're right. Some cats are born hunters. But it won't be like that in heaven. In heaven, neither people or animals will hurt each other."

Patrick looked at his shovel and at the tiny army of ants still marching down the sidewalk. "Are you like Fluffy?" Grandma asked. "Are *you* going to eat these ants?"

Patrick giggled. "No way," he said. "So I guess I shouldn't smash them either."

"Right," Grandma said. "Now why don't you and your shovel find something really fun to do?"

"Like building a sand castle?" Patrick guessed.

"Exactly," Grandma said. "Come on. I'll race you to the sandbox!"—V.L.K.

Do Not Complain

Do not complain against one another. James 5:9, TEV.

"Jack's always breaking things!" Harry cried, glaring at his broken car.

Mother frowned. "Why are you boys always fighting?"

"He takes my stuff," Harry complained. "And he breaks it."

Jack sniffled, and big tears came to his eyes. Harry turned to Mother. "I can't help it that he's smaller than I am."

Mother shook her head. "Jack can't help it either. He's only 2 years old." She looked at Harry. "Don't you remember what we said about sharing your toys?"

"I remember," Harry said. "But it isn't fair."

Mother looked at Harry, then at little Jack. "Jack shares his toys with you."

His baby brother smiled and held out his ABC book. "But those are baby things," Harry said. "I'm too big for baby things."

Mother smiled again. "Then you're too big to complain."

"Too big to complain?" Harry repeated.

"That's right," Mother said. "God wants us to help one another. To love one another. Not to complain."

Harry looked at his baby brother. "I do love Jack," he said. "Only I don't like it when he breaks my things."

Mother gave Harry a hug. "I know," she said. "Let's put them up where he can't reach them."

"OK," Harry said. He smiled at Mother. "But first, let's give Jack a hug too."—N.C.P.

Truly Sorry

I confess my sins; I am sorry for what I have done. Ps. 38:18, TLB.

"Now you watch the little ones, Mary Lou, while I help Pa out in the field for the next couple hours," Amanda said firmly. Amanda and Tiffany were having such fun playing "olden times" in the backyard. They were dressed in long skirts with bonnets on their heads. The walls of their pretend sod house were made of branches. Marigold petals cooked nicely in their make-believe soup. And at all times the pioneer family had to watch out for pretend "wild animals," for Stella, the collie, and Amber, the cat, might show up without warning.

The girls could have played happily for quite a time if it hadn't been for the interruption of Amanda's younger brother, Jeremy. "Jeremy, don't ride your tricycle through our house," Amanda scolded. "You're messing it up!"

"You girls are just playing a dumb game," Jeremy grumbled as he tipped over the pot of "soup" and broke out the back wall of the house.

"I'm telling Mom," cried Amanda.

Jeremy knew he was in trouble because Mom wouldn't let him get away with destroying the girls' things on purpose. All of a sudden he felt very sorry.

"Jeremy, I believe you are sorry for being unkind to Amanda and Tiffany," Mom said seriously, "but it's not enough just to tell me you're sorry. After you have apologized to the girls, come back in, and we'll ask Jesus to forgive you too. Only Jesus can help you not to act that way again. You must stay inside for the rest of the day, too. Maybe that will help you remember not to do it again."

Jeremy spent a long, boring afternoon in the house when he wanted to be playing outside. He felt really and truly sorry when he realized that he *could* have been playing the pioneer daddy in the girls' pioneer house, or he *could* have pretended to be a brave hunter that protected the family from bears. Staying inside was no fun at all!—P.M.M.

Wait for Me

Ask, and it shall be given you. Matt. 7:7.

"It's stopped snowing," Katie's older brother, Mitch said. "Can I go sledding now?"

"Me too!" Katie begged.

Mom looked out the window. "Yes, it will do you both good to get some fresh air," she told them. "Katie, wear your boots and mittens."

Katie ran to her room. She found one red boot in the closet and sat down and put it on. Then she looked around for its mate. She saw toys on the floor, but no boot. Katie looked under the bed. She found her teddy bear, but no boot.

"Come on, Katie," Mitch yelled. "I'm ready to go."

"Wait for me!" Katie cried. "I can't find my other boot."

Mitch came to her door. "If you'd put away all the things that are on your floor, you'd be able to find it," he said.

Katie almost cried. "That would take forever," she said. "Will you wait for me? Please."

Mitch pulled off his mittens. "I'll do something even better," he said. "I'll help you search."

A few minutes later the room was almost clean. But they still hadn't found the boot. *Where could it be?* Katie thought as she put the last of her toys into the toy box and closed the lid. Then she saw something behind the toy box.

"My boot! We found it!" Katie called as she pulled it on and ran to get her coat. "Thanks for helping me," she told Mitch as they ran out the door. "You're a neat brother."

"Well, you helped me find my lost book," Mitch said. He grabbed the rope on his sled. "Come on. When we get to the hill, you can ride down with me."

Katie tucked her mittened hand in his, and they left a trail of footprints in the new snow. —M.H.D.

The Parade

My son, do not walk in the way with them, keep your foot from their path. Prov. 1:15, NKJV.

"The parade is coming! The parade is coming! I hear the drums, I hear the music, I see the people. The parade is coming!" Jumping up and down, 5-year-old Sonny looked out the door of his father's store waiting for the parade to pass right by him. Oh, how he loved the sound of the trumpets and the drums, the bright costumes, and the clowns. The closer the parade came the more excited Sonny became. He wished he could march in a parade.

Soon the parade was marching right by his father's store. Sonny watched the marchers with big, excited eyes. Some carried flags, and some were playing the drums. Clowns ran up and down near the people who watched from the sidewalk. Dogs barked, people cheered, and children sat high on their parents' shoulders so they could see everything.

Sonny was so excited about the parade passing by that before he knew it he was marching right behind the parade. He followed it all the way across town until finally the parade was over. And Sonny was a long way from his father's store.

Sonny had a long walk back to the store, and he got very tired. When he finally reached home, he discovered that his parents had been very worried about him. "I'm sorry," Sonny told them. "I didn't mean to follow the parade for so long. It was just so much fun that I didn't know how far I was going."

"You must never leave home like that without asking," Daddy told him. *"Never!* Do you understand?"

Sonny nodded his head. "I promise," he said. And he kept that promise. —C.B.T.

The Right Thing to Do

What you say affects how you live. You will be rewarded by how you speak. Prov. 18:20, ICB.

"Hello, my name is Eddie," the new girl told the group of children standing near the school swings.

"Eddie is a boy's name," the short boy said. He and his boyfriends laughed.

"Well, my name is Eddie, and I'm a girl. So Eddie is a girl's name, too," Eddie said and smiled.

The boys laughed louder.

"Eddie *is* a boy's name," a tall girl said. She stood with her arms crossed, facing Eddie.

"Eddie is a very good name for a girl, too," Eddie replied. She opened her book bag and pulled out a writing tablet. She held it up so everyone could see the name printed in fancy letters at the top of the page. The letters spelled out Eddie Patricia Green.

"That's a neat tablet!" the short boy said.

"I'll call you Patricia," the tall girl told Eddie.

"Oh, no, thank you," Eddie replied. "I want everyone to know that I'm named after my dad."

Suddenly the tall girl smiled. "Well, Miss Eddie Green," she said, "my name is Samantha. I'm named after *my* dad, and you can call me Sam."

Then the other children began telling Eddie their names. Whitley (WIT-lee) was named after a famous gospel singer. Denene (De-NEEN) said that her name was a combination of her older sisters' names, Dorthene and Arlene. Sam's brother, Jacqmel (JOCK-mel), even taught Eddie how to pronounce his name. And the children had a good time playing together until their teacher rang the bell, calling them to morning classes.

What do you think would have happened if Eddie had talked angrily when the children teased her? How was Eddie rewarded for speaking in a friendly way?—F.J.C.

Latchkey Grandma

For I will have respect unto you. Lev. 26:9, KJV.

Terry and his sister Tanna pressed their noses to the window and stared out. Where, oh where, was Grandma? Terry felt funny inside. Ever since Grandma came to stay with them, he'd been so busy with his friend next door that he didn't spend much time with Grandma. Sure, he loved her, but Tommy had a brand new VCR and a whole bunch of neat videos Terry hadn't seen. Besides, Grandma would be there a whole month.

"Good! There she is," Tanna said. She ran to the front door and threw it open before Grandma could get out her key. "Grandma, where have you been?"

Grandma's eyes looked sad. "I'll tell you later." And no matter how much the children teased, they couldn't make her change her mind.

After dinner Tanna reminded Grandma, "You said you'd tell us where you were all afternoon."

Grandma didn't smile at all, and Terry felt even funnier than ever when she said, "I went and bought a bus ticket so I could go home."

"But you're supposed to stay with us a lot longer!" Terry burst out. Mom and Tanna agreed, and Mom looked shocked.

Grandma shook her head. "I don't like being a latchkey grandma. I want to go home where I have my dog and cat there with me. It's too lonely with all of you gone all day."

Terry felt awful. Why hadn't he stayed with Grandma? "Please stay," he begged. "We really want you. I won't go over to Tommy's anymore."

While Grandma was thinking about it, Terry and Tanna put their heads together and came up with a lot of different things they thought Grandma would like to do. And guess what! Grandma decided to stay.

Have you ever thought that grandparents can get lonely? Well, they can. What do your grandmother and grandfather enjoy doing when they visit you?—C.L.R.

The Heart-shaped Cookie

Look at the birds in the sky; they do not sow and reap and store in barns, yet your heavenly Father feeds them. Matt. 6:26, REB.

Laura made something special for her elderly neighbor for Valentine's Day. It was a huge frosted heart-shaped cookie. And she pressed a sunburst of walnuts into the center and a whole row of raisins around the edge.

Mama wrapped it in plastic while Laura got on her coat and mittens.

"Come here," Mama said, tying Laura's hood snugly.

Ice crackled under Laura's boots. She started skipping. Suddenly she lost her balance on the slippery sidewalk. The heart-shaped cookie flipped up into the air and crashed down into a pile of crumbs. Laura felt as crushed as the cookie.

Mrs. Domres was expecting Laura, and a moment later she opened the door. "Come in, dear, it's freezing," she called.

Laura burst into sobs. "I made you a heart-shaped cookie, all decorated, but I dropped it on the way. It's just a big waste now!"

Mrs. Domres hugged Laura and tried to soothe her. "Love is never wasted, Laura," she said, pointing out the window. "Look."

There on the walkway, enjoying a feast of heart-shaped cookie crumbs, were three hungry sparrows, two shivering robins, and a squawking blue jay. Two starlings waddled in for a bite, and several shy finches eyed the scene from a distance, waiting to snatch their share. Laura saw Mrs. Domres' glowing expression as she watched a pert chickadee steal in to grab a crumb.

"Love is never wasted," Laura said. And in spite of herself, she smiled.—V.L.K.

Ask, and You Will Receive

Ask, and you will receive; seek, and you will find; knock, and the door will be opened to you. Luke 11:9, TEV.

Judy stared at the Christmas tree, but its bright lights were all blurred. There was no new bike under it.

She swallowed to keep from crying. The Sabbath school teacher was wrong. She'd said that God would answer prayers. Judy had prayed and prayed for a new bike. The old one was dented and rusty. It had been Sue's before it was hers, and Judy really wanted a new one of her own. But God hadn't answered her prayers. There was no bike under the tree.

The next time the Sabbath school teacher started to talk about prayer, Judy raised her hand. "It doesn't work," she said. "Prayer doesn't work."

"What makes you say that?" the teacher asked.

"I prayed and prayed," Judy told her. "But I didn't get the bike I wanted."

The teacher smiled. "You asked God for a bike?" she asked kindly.

"Yes," Judy said. "I asked and asked, but I didn't get it. God doesn't answer prayers."

The teacher looked at the class. "I know that makes you feel sad," she told Judy. "But that doesn't mean that God didn't answer your prayer."

"But—"

"When you ask your mother for a cookie, does she always give you one?"

Judy frowned. "No-o-o," she said slowly. "Once, when I was little, I ate too many and got sick. Sometimes she tells me to wait till supper."

The teacher nodded. "It's that way with God, too. Sometimes God tells you to wait. But we know one thing for sure—if you ask to belong to God, to have God with you, that prayer will always be answered."—N.C.P.

Protecting the Earth

God placed . . . man in the Garden . . . to cultivate and guard it. Gen. 2:15, TEV.

"I'll beat you to the creek," shouted Jody to her friend Michele. Off the girls ran toward the woods at the back of

Jody's house. The girls loved playing in the woods, and today would be extra-special because Mama had made a yummy picnic lunch.

Mama sat on a blanket in the sunshine reading while the girls played follow the leader. Michele almost fell into the water when they crossed the small stream on a log, so she suggested they play something different.

About that time Mama called, "Be ready to eat in five minutes."

"Let's pick a bouquet of flowers for our picnic," Michele suggested.

In the open place next to the woods hundreds of purple, yellow, and white flowers brightly bloomed among the green grass. Suddenly the girls stopped. Right at their feet bloomed a yellow orchid-like flower. Quickly Michele reached down to pick it.

"Don't pick it!" Jody shouted so loudly that Michele jumped. Jody was only 4 years old, and they weren't used to hearing her talk like that. "Mama's told me not to pick a flower if there are only a few of them. Mama says if I don't help protect the earth, who will?"

And so after they ate lunch, they took Mama back to see the pretty yellow flower. "I'm proud of you, Jody, for remembering what I'd told you about taking care of the earth."

Jody's mama was right. Even though you are small, you can do your part in protecting the earth. God created the earth beautiful and perfect but people have treated the earth carelessly, especially during the past 100 years.

Here are some ideas of what you can do to "guard" the earth. *(Maybe you and your family can think of some more.)* Always throw away trash rather than dropping it on the ground. Recycle papers, bottles, and cans. Don't destroy flowers and other wildlife unless you absolutely have to! Let's keep the earth the best we can until Jesus comes again!—P.M.M.

A Push and a Shove—
A Mission Story

The angel of the Lord encamps all around those who fear Him, and delivers them. Ps. 34:7, NKJV.

It was dark! The missionary family had been riding all day on the dusty roads traveling to their new house. Everyone was hot, hungry, dusty, and tired. Their little Volkswagen was packed full with suitcases, books, food, and the family dog. The windows were rolled down, and the road dust blew over everybody. There weren't any motels so they could stop and sleep. And there were no lights to brighten the road. All they had were the lights from their car.

Daddy kept on driving. He hoped they'd come to a city and find a motel so they could rest for the night. Suddenly they came to a great big muddy place in the road. There was nothing to do but go through it. Daddy drove slowly and carefully, but all of a sudden the car stopped. It was stuck! Daddy tried to get the car out, but the more he tried, the more the tires dug deeper and deeper into the mud. There were no other cars on the road, so no one was there to help them. What could they do to get out of the mud?

The boys were asleep in the back seat but Donna-Maria was still awake. Daddy sat behind the steering wheel, trying to give the car enough power to make it out. Mommy and Donna-Maria were very quiet. They bowed their heads and asked God to please help them. Donna-Maria was afraid of spending the night on the dark road. While they were still praying, they felt something bump the car hard from behind, and they started going forward. Soon they were out of the mud and on dry ground. Who had helped them? Daddy got out of the car to look, but no one was there. "God has answered our prayers," Mother said. "He sent angels to push our car out of the mud."

The happy family continued their trip and finally reached their new home. Many times the family talked about the angels who came and pushed and shoved their little Volkswagen out of the mud on that dark, lonely road.—C.B.T.

What a Pest!

As I have loved you, so you are to love one another. John 13:34, REB.

Gemma and her friend Tally were playing house. Mama opened the door and brought baby Lissy into Gemma's room.

"Keep this child in here for a few minutes, Gemma," Mama said. "She woke up early from her nap, and I haven't finished waxing the kitchen floor yet. You know she doesn't like being alone." Mama put Lissy down and closed the door.

Lissy looked at Gemma and Tally. Then she saw the toy dishes set out on the little table. Lissy toddled over to the table as fast as her little fat legs would go.

"No, Lissy!" Gemma cried as Lissy threw the dishes on the floor.

"What a pest!" Tally said, making a face. "I'm glad I don't have a little sister."

When Gemma took the dishes away, Lissy toddled over to the bookcase. She laughed and began to pull the books from the shelves.

"No, Lissy!" Gemma rescued her favorite book. "Here. Play with this doll."

"What a pest!" Tally said, picking up her own doll so Lissy wouldn't grab it. "Don't you wish you were an only child like me?"

"No." Gemma sat down on the floor. She pulled Lissy into her lap. "Sometimes I get mad when Lissy gets into my things or is bad and breaks something. But I'm glad she's my little sister. I love Lissy."

(NOTE TO READERS: Talk about why Gemma loved Lissy even though she was sometimes a "pest.")—M.H.D.

A Real Job

Commit your work to the Lord, then it will succeed. Prov. 16:3, TLB.

"How would you like a job, Bethy?" Mom asked.

Bethy looked surprised. "You mean for money?"

Mom nodded. "My citrus trees need to be watered every day now that it's hot. I'll pay you 50 cents each day."

Bethy jumped to her feet. "Yes. I want to do it. I'll get lots of money."

Mom took Bethy out on the sunny deck where six trees planted in six big pots stayed during the summer. She told Bethy to use the hose and to be sure to give each tree lots and lots of water every day. She said to fill the big pots all the way to the top three times every time she watered.

Bethy was excited when she started her job. But after a few days it wasn't fun anymore. Every day she hurried faster, giving each tree just a little water.

One day Mom noticed the citrus leaves turning yellow. Then the leaves started falling off. "I wonder what's going wrong with the trees," she said.

Bethy couldn't tell a lie. "I'm not giving them enough water," she said. "I'll go give them some more right now. And I won't forget after this."

The Bible tells us that no matter what we do, we should do the very best job we can. The Bible says that whatever work we do we should do it for Jesus. That means that we're not doing it just for Mom. We're doing it for Jesus, too. — V.W.

Crack-headed Janette

For the Son of man is come to save that which was lost. Matt. 18:11, KJV.

All afternoon Kristen and her little brother Rudy played outdoors in the billows of snow. They made snow angels and snow people. When Dad got home from work he laughed and said, "Washington State is in for an old-fashioned hard winter. We'll probably have snow on the ground until spring."

"Oh, boy!" Rudy shouted and raced through the white blanket on the ground.

Not Kristen. She ran inside and burst into tears. "Mom, I can't find Janette," she cried. Of all her dolls, Kristen loved Janette best.

"Where did you leave her?" Mom asked.

"I don't know," Kristen cried. "I had her earlier."

"Maybe she's out in the snowstorm," Rudy said when he came in after it had started snowing really hard. But all their searching didn't find Janette.

Dad was right. It snowed, stopped, and snowed again. Christmas came, and Kristen got a beautiful doll that she named Ruth, but she still missed Janette, the very first doll she had ever had.

Months passed and spring came. The ground popped back into sight after a warm wind which the Indians call a chinook. One day Rudy rushed into the house. "I found Janette!" he called, holding out the doll. But her china face had cracks, and the stuffing had come out of her body. "Poor crack-headed Janette," Rudy said.

Mom stuffed Janette again and put a new cap on her. Kristen still loved Janette best, but she loved Jesus and her family even more. —C.L.R.

Consensed from *Primary Treasure* story, May 14, 1988.

Finders, Givers

So, when you give alms, do not announce it with a flourish of trumpets. . . . Your good deed must be in secret, and your Father who sees what is done in secret will reward you. Matt. 6:2-4, REB.

Mama, Pierre, and Cecile were shopping for winter hats and mittens. Suddenly Mama said, "I don't believe my eyes!" and picked up a $50 bill.

The children's eyes lit up as well.

"Can I get a new doll?" Cecile asked.

"I want a new football," Pierre said.

"Stop!" Mama laughed. "This money isn't even ours."

She took the bill to the store manager. He took Mama's name and phone number and said, "If no one claims it in a week, it's yours."

The store manager called Mama the following week. She took Pierre and Cecile to pick up the money. It was very cold out, so they wore the hats and mittens they'd bought last week.

"We're rich!" Pierre and Cecile had ideas for the money. Mama had other ideas. They stopped at the post office. Mama put the money into an envelope and sent it to the Graham family.

"Why?" asked Pierre.

"Because," said Mama, "the Grahams are laid off from their jobs at the factory. They need the money more than we do. Maybe they'll be able to buy hats and mittens for their children. I've seen the children out in the cold without hats."

"But why didn't you sign your name, Mama?" Cecile had seen the note. "They won't know who sent it."

"They don't need to know. We know, and God knows. That's enough for me," Mama said.

They left the post office to walk home.

Pierre and Cecile felt the warmth of their hats and mittens as the bitter wind blew.

"Enough for us, too," they decided together.—V.L.K.

Special Gifts

Each one . . . must use for the good of others the special gift he has received from God. 1 Peter 4:10, TEV.

Mandy stared at the pretty fallen leaves. She liked leaves and she liked raking them. She stooped and took a fuzzy brown caterpillar to a safe spot in the hedge. Then she went back to raking—and frowning.

It was report card day. Why couldn't she do better in school? She tried. She tried really hard.

She picked up another brown ball of caterpillar and took it to the hedge with the other. She liked to think that in the spring they would turn into something pretty.

Mandy sighed. She wasn't pretty like her big sister Sue. Or smart like her bigger sister Peggy. To be pretty and smart were their special gifts. God must have forgotten her. *She* didn't have a special gift.

"Want some help?" Grandpa asked, coming down from the back porch.

"Sure," Mandy said. It was Grandpa who'd taught her to watch out for the caterpillars.

"Something bothering you?" Grandpa asked, starting to rake. "That's the biggest frown I've ever seen."

Mandy tried to smile. "It's me, Grandpa. I don't have a special gift from God."

Grandpa stopped raking. "Wherever did you get an idea like that?"

"It's true," Mandy said. "I'm not smart like Peggy or pretty like Sue."

Grandpa shrugged. "Pretty and smart aren't everything."

"But I'm not *anything,*" Mandy said, bending for another caterpillar.

Grandpa snorted. "Nonsense, girl. You've got the best gift of all."

Mandy put the caterpillar with the others. "Me?" she asked. "What kind of gift do I have?"

"The gift of caring," Grandpa said. "You care about God's creatures. You care about other people."

Mandy thought about that. "But I'm supposed to do that. Jesus said so."

Grandpa nodded. "That's right. But God's made it easier for you and me. He gave us the gift of caring."

He leaned his rake against a tree and gave Mandy a big hug. "Our gift is one of the best."—N.C.P.

God's Super Tree— A Mission Story

The righteous shall flourish like the palm tree. Psalm 92:12, KJV.

Where I live in Borneo, I see many tall palm trees that do not have branches. Their trunks grow up, up, higher than the houses. Way up at the top of the trees, big leaves that look like feathers spread out in all directions. We call these leaves fronds. And among the leaves grow many large, round fruits called coconuts.

You could never count the ways that the coconut palm helps people. If you break open the tough coconut shell, you find creamy white, sweet-tasting meat and clear, cool, sweet water. Lots of people like to drink it. The people use the husk that grows around the nut to make mats to sit on and ropes for tying things. They also use it to make fans that help keep them cool and brooms for sweeping their floors.

Can you imagine sleeping on a bed made from a coconut tree? How about taking a bath with soap made from the rich coconut oil?

The people in Borneo even build their houses and make most of their furniture from the coconut palm. And that's not all. The tree offers people cooling shade, and the wood to cook their food. Oil squeezed from the coconut meat also lights their lamps. From this tree the fisherman makes his boat, sails, fishing line, and nets. Even when strong winds blow, the coconut palm stands firm. Its roots grow down deep.

The coconut palm is one of the most useful trees in the world. In the same way, God wants to help you be useful, too. When you invite Jesus into your heart, He will fill you with His love so you can be helpful to others. Won't you ask Jesus to make you strong, beautiful, and useful like the palm tree?—E.E.L.

Sticks, Stones, and the Apple Tree

And I say to you, ask, and it will be given to you. Luke 11:9, NKJV.

"Throw the rock higher, Sue, and try to hit that big red apple way up there on the top branch."

Sue and her brother Allen were in the yard next door throwing rocks and sticks at the apples on the apple tree. If only they could knock one apple off the tree. The apple Sue was trying to hit seemed like it was glued to the tree. There the apple sat—shining in the sun, big, red, and ready to eat.

Allen found a larger stone and threw it at the apple, but he missed. Sue picked up a big stone and tried to hit the apple again. She missed.

If I throw the stone a little more to the right, thought Sue, *I think I could hit the apple this time.* Looking way up at the apple, Sue threw the stone as hard as she could. Oh! The stone missed the apple, but it hit something else—the neighbor's bedroom window. With a loud crash, the window broke. Poor Sue; she knew the neighbor was going to tell Daddy. And she was right.

Daddy called Sue and Allen into the living room as soon as he came into the house from work. He asked them if they had been throwing stones at the apples, trying to knock them off the neighbor's tree. They nodded their heads and said, "Yes." Daddy then asked them about the broken window. Who had thrown the stone that had broken the bedroom window?

Sue looked down at the floor, and with tears running down her face, she said quietly, "I did, Daddy. I broke the window."

"You know it was wrong to go into the neighbor's yard and knock apples off her tree without getting permission," Daddy said.

Sue and Allen nodded.

Daddy said that he was going to spank them for trying to get apples without first asking their neighbor. He said that was the same as stealing.

Later Sue and Allen went next door and told the neighbor they were sorry for throwing stones at her apples and were also sorry for breaking her window.

Now when someone talks about sticks, stones, and apple trees, Sue and Allen remember the spanking they got, and how much nicer it is to ask for the things they may want. — C.B.T.

Empty Pockets

If sinners entice you, do not consent. Prov. 1:10, RSV.

Joby liked going to K Mart with Daddy. "I need to show you something," Joby said. He pulled Daddy down the aisle to the toy department. They stopped in front of a display of miniature Matchbox cars, and Joby picked up a tiny blue racecar.

"Will you buy this for me?" he asked.

"Not today," Daddy said. "Your birthday is coming soon. You never know what might happen on your birthday, so you'd better put it back for now." And Daddy went across the aisle to the Automotive Department.

Joby held the little blue racer for a long time. He really wanted that car. And his birthday was a whole month away.

"Take it out of the plastic box and put the car in your pocket," a voice whispered. Joby spun around and saw an older boy standing next to him.

"Go ahead," the boy said in a low voice. "Just open the package from the back and take the car out of the plastic box. It's easy."

"But that's stealing," Joby whispered.

142

"This is a big store. They won't miss a few cars." The boy grinned. "I've got a couple in my pocket right now."

Joby looked hard at the boy's pocket. The cars were so tiny they didn't even make a lump.

"Do it." The boy gave Joby a nudge with his elbow. "Nobody will know." Joby stared at the tiny blue car. Suddenly his heart began to pound hard against his chest. He could hardly breathe.

"I will know and God will know," Joby said. His hand was shaking as he dropped the package back on the shelf. "I'm never going to steal anything. Not ever."

Joby rushed to find Daddy. He was glad that his pockets were empty.—M.H.D.

Are You a Good Neighbor?

Love your neighbor as you love yourself. Matt. 22:39, TEV.

Good neighbors show their love to those who live around them. Here are some ways that they show love.

Being friendly by
* Smiling at their neighbors.
* Speaking when they meet their neighbors.
* Treating the neighbors' moms and dads as kindly as they'd want the neighbors to treat their own moms and dads.

Being helpful by
* Keeping the neighborhood or the apartment building beautiful by picking up trash, even if they didn't throw it down.
* Not letting their dogs or cats play in neighbors' yards, and cleaning up after their pets.
* Returning the neighbor's newspaper if their dog takes it to play with.
* Being quiet around a neighbor's house or apartment.

Sharing by

* Giving Sabbath school papers to their neighbors, but not just leaving them in the hallway for the janitor to clean up.
* Giving cookies that their mom has made.
* Teaching their neighbors songs.
* Telling Bible stories and nature stories.

Are you a good neighbor? Tell a story about how you have been a good neighbor.—F.J.C.

Noises in the Night

God is our refuge and strength, an ever-present help in trouble. Ps. 46:1, NIV.

Chris clutched the blanket and pulled it over his head. It didn't help. The strange noise that sounded so loud in the dark night went on. A kind of *whirrr, shirr.* What could it be? He'd carefully closed the window before he went to bed. He knew Dad had locked the door to the old house they were staying in for vacation. Nothing could have gotten in, could it?

Whirr, shirr. Chris held his breath and tiptoed from his bedroom into the living room. A big wood stove sat at one side of the room. If it turned cold, a fire would feel good, but for now it just sat there, black and cold. The noise sounded like it came from there.

Should he wake up Dad?

Chris shook his head. No. Dad needed sleep. He'd been so tired lately. The last thing he needed was for Chris to wake him up in the middle of the night.

"Please, God, help me not to be afraid. Whatever's in there can't get out. Or if I'm just imagining it, please help me go to sleep." It took a long time, but Chris finally settled down and slept.

The next morning Dad called a sleepy boy. "Wake up, Chris. Come see what I found."

Chris leaped from bed. Dad had gently removed a small bat that had somehow flown down the chimney and gotten into the cold stove. Chris laughed. He was glad to know what the noises in the night had been!—C.L.R.

Miracles

Thomas said, "My Lord and my God!" Jesus said to him, "Because you have seen me you have found faith. Happy are they who find faith without seeing me." John 20:28, 29, REB.

Hannah and Mama were walking in a nearby field. Hannah said, "Mama, I wish Jesus was alive today so I could see a miracle right before my eyes."

Mama said, "Jesus is alive, Hannah. He's in heaven. When He was on earth, He performed miracles for the people who didn't believe He was God's Son. We don't need miracles to believe in Him today."

"Still," said Hannah, "I wish . . ."

They walked on. Hannah kept looking for a miracle. Instead she found a caterpillar's hard chrysalis hanging from a milkweed plant. They picked Queen Anne's lace and chicory blossoms and listened to birds singing. Suddenly Mama said, "Look!"

A hard, dry chrysalis was changing. It was splitting apart! Hannah and Mama stood without saying a word. They were so quiet that they were hardly breathing. They just watched and waited.

At last a wrinkled creature struggled out. Its tiny feet grasped its broken chrysalis and rested on it. Its wings were tightly wrapped around its body.

After several minutes its wings began to unfold. Slowly they spread into a delicate pattern of fresh bright orange, snowy white, and velvety black.

The newborn butterfly flicked its fragile body, fluttered its wings, and took to the air, floating like a flower petal on a gentle breeze.

Mama gasped, "A monarch butterfly!"

Hannah sighed, "A miracle!"

Have you ever seen a "miracle"?—V.L.K.

The Things That Are in Heaven

You have been raised to life with Christ, so set your hearts on the things that are in heaven. Col. 3:1, TEV.

"Look, Mother!" Becky called. "That's what I want!"

Mother looked up from her papers. "That's a nice playhouse, Becky."

Becky clapped her hands. "Oh, good!" she said, for more than anything in the world she wanted a bright-red-and-yellow playhouse. The one in the picture had doors and windows that opened and a telephone on the wall. "Then I can have one?" she asked.

Mother shook her head. "No, Becky, I'm afraid not."

"But I want it!"

Mother put down her pen. "We can't just have everything we want, honey. You have quite a few toys."

Becky frowned. "But all my friends have playhouses."

Mother put her papers aside. "Come here," she said.

Becky climbed into Mother's lap. "It's like this," Mother said. "We belong to Jesus. We've asked Him into our hearts. Your daddy and I must be careful with the money Jesus helps us make. We must spend it only for things that are really important."

Becky sighed. "But a playhouse is important."

Mother gave her a hug. "I know, honey. It's important to sweet little girls like you. But you have lots of toys and the playhouse is expensive. Besides that, it's made of plastic which just breaks and clutters up God's earth."

Becky gave a big sigh. "You know, Becky," Mother said, "we could use the money we'd spend on the playhouse to help people who don't have jobs and are hungry."

Becky thought about that. She remembered the day she'd missed lunch. Being hungry hurt.

"God wants us to be good and kind," Mother said. "He helps us care about His earth and about other people."

146

Becky didn't understand it all, but she could see it wouldn't be a good idea to have God's earth all covered with plastic playhouses. And she knew being hungry was just awful.

She gave Mother a big hug. "Can we feed a lot of children with the money?"

"Yes," Mother said with a smile. "A lot."—N.C.P.

Helping

She has done what she could. Mark 14:8, NKJV.

Ring . . . ring . . . Five-year-old Amy listened as Mom answered the phone. "Oh, that will be wonderful," Amy heard Mom say. Mom hung up the phone and called for all the children to come.

"That was Aunt Lela, and guess what? Aunt Lela, Uncle Rich, and your cousins are coming early this afternoon to stay for the weekend. Isn't that great! I need good helpers so we'll be ready for them. Then all you kids can play for a while before supper."

Oldest brother Jeff went to the garage to start the lawn mower. Middle brother Steve pulled out the vacuum. David, the youngest brother, picked up rugs from each room and took them outside to shake. As Amy watched her mom cooking and her older brothers doing their jobs, she wondered, *"What can I do to help?"*

Suddenly she had a thought. "Mama, can I dust?" Amy asked.

"Sure, but let me take off the antique bowl and the breakable items in the living room," Mom told her.

Very carefully Amy moved the plant off the end table. Next she took off the bookends. Finally she lifted up the special book of poems and placed it on the couch. Amy carefully dusted each furniture piece with a soft white cloth. When she finished the living room, on she went to the family room. Her arm got a little tired, but she had just one more room. She couldn't stop now.

"Oh, Amy," Mom exclaimed, "you've done such a nice job. Thank you."

That afternoon Amy had fun playing with her cousins. She felt especially happy. Although she was little, she had done her part.

What can you do today to help your mother or daddy? How have you helped in the past?—P.M.M.

A Tap on the Shoulder

And the angel of His Presence saved them. Isa. 63:9, NKJV.

Scott had to cross two very busy streets to get to the bread store. Each time Mother sent him to buy bread, she would say the same thing. "Scott, be careful when you cross the streets."

One morning Scott's mother told Scott that she needed bread again. "Be careful when you cross the streets," she told him. He was whistling a song he'd learned in Sabbath school when he came to the busy streets he had to cross. Before stepping into the street, Scott looked to the right and then to the left to see if any cars were coming. When he saw that no cars were coming, he walked across the street to the other side.

Now, he had one more street to cross before he got to the store. Again, Scott looked to the left and to the right. Just as he was ready to step off the sidewalk into the street, Scott felt a tap on his shoulder. Thinking it was a friend, Scott stepped back on the sidewalk and looked around to see who had touched him. No sooner had he stepped back than a car raced past him from around the corner. And *nobody else* was there!

Scott went to the store, bought the bread, came home, and told his mother what had happened. Mother smiled and said, "Scott, I believe your guardian angel touched you to keep you from crossing the street. You didn't know a car would be coming from around the corner, but your angel did, and your angel didn't want you to get hit. That's why we pray and ask Jesus to send His angels to take care of us." Scott and Mother prayed and thanked Jesus right there in the kitchen for keeping Scott from being hit by the car. —C.B.T.

The Tulip Mystery

Know the truth, and the truth will set you free. John 8:32, NIV.

Darrell came outside to play with Wags in his baby-sitter's front yard. Soon the dog got tired of playing and ran into the backyard. Darrell pulled his wagon along the walk. As he got near the flower bed, he saw something red in the grass. It was a pretty tulip without a stem. He picked it up and put it in his wagon. As he walked along, he found more tulips in the grass, so picked them up too.

Suddenly the screen door slammed and his baby-sitter, Mrs. Todd, rushed toward him. "Darrell, look what you've done to my beautiful tulips," she scolded.

"I didn't pick them," Darrell said. "I found them in the grass."

Mrs. Todd put her hands on her hips. "Don't lie, Darrell. You're the only one here. Now go into the house and sit in the time-out chair. Think about what you've done."

Darrell trudged into the house. He sat in the chair by the window and looked out.

I didn't pick the tulips, Darrell thought. He leaned his chin on his hands. *I'm being punished for something I didn't do.*

Wags came trotting into the front yard on his short legs. He looked around. Then he trotted over to the flower bed, reached up, and bit off a tulip.

"Mrs. Todd, come quick!" Darrell cried. "Look! Look out the window!"

"What's wrong?" Mrs. Todd got there in time to see Wags bite off the next tulip. "Well, what do you know?" she said in surprise. "I'm sorry I didn't believe you. Wags is the guilty one."

"Can I go outside and play now?" Darrell asked.

"Yes, of course," she answered. "But first, will you forgive me? You've never lied to me before, and I should have believed you."

Darrell gave her a big smile, and Mrs. Todd rushed outside to save the rest of the tulips.—M.H.D.

Be Forgiving

If you forgive others the wrong they have done to you, your Father in heaven will forgive you. Matt. 6:14, TEV.

"I hate you!" Sally yelled. "You broke my best doll!" Sally wanted to cry. She felt so bad; she wanted to make Jane feel bad too. Jane was always playing with her toys and always breaking them.

"I'm sorry," Jane said. There were big tears in her eyes. But Sally was glad. She wanted Jane to feel bad.

"Please," Jane said, "I didn't mean to break your doll."

"Yes, you did," Sally cried. "Go home. I don't want to play with you."

Jane looked like she was going to say something else; then she gulped and ran out.

Sally went to the kitchen to help Mother with supper.

"Can I use the pretty dishes?" she asked.

Mother nodded. "Just be careful."

"I will." Sally liked the pretty dishes. "Mother, Jane broke my best doll," she said.

"That's too bad," Mother said, looking up from the soup she was stirring. "Maybe we can fix your doll."

"We can't—" Sally began. She turned in a hurry and her elbow hit a plate, knocking it off the table. The plate hit the floor with a crash. Pieces flew everywhere.

"Oh, no!" Sally cried. "I broke it! Oh, Mother, your pretty plate. Please forgive me."

Mother frowned. "Did you forgive Jane for breaking your doll?"

Sally shook her head. "No."

"Then I don't know if I should forgive you." Mother looked at Sally. "You didn't forgive Jane."

Sally hung her head. "Should I forgive her?"

"Yes," Mother said. "God wants us to forgive each other. So I'll forgive you for breaking my plate."

"And I'll forgive Jane," Sally cried. "That will make God happy."—N.C.P.

The Caver and the Knocker

Listen to your father. Prov. 23:22, NIV.

Rudy lived in a big house several miles from a small town. He didn't always have other children to play with, so he made his own fun. One thing he really enjoyed was taking old boards and pretending to be a carpenter.

"Be careful of those boards," Dad warned Rudy one night. "I'll help you build a playhouse when I can, but I'm too busy right now."

"It's OK, Dad. I can build a caver and a knocker."

"A what?"

"A caver and a knocker." Rudy always made up unusual names for what he built. So while Dad pushed the big lawn mower over the bumpy yard, Rudy put boards together and sang over and over, "Oh, my caver and my knocker. My caver and my knocker."

He played with his "building" for the next few days. Then one day he came into the house and sat down in a chair. He didn't say a word.

"Why aren't you outdoors?" Dad asked.

"I don't have anything to do."

Dad looked surprised. "What happened to your caver and your knocker?"

Rudy squirmed around. He rubbed a bump on his head and said, "Uh, it caved in and knocked me on the head!"

Daddy sighed. "Hey, I'm sorry I've been too busy to help you with your playhouse," he said. "I know it's not easy working alone."

And so, as soon as Dad could, he helped Rudy saw some boards, nail them together, and Rudy finally had a playhouse that didn't fall down. —C.L.R.

Grandpa and the Geese

But ask the beasts, and they will teach you; ask the birds of the air to inform you. Job 12:7, REB.

"Grandpa, are you coming to church today?" Mandy asked.

Grandpa poured more grain into the cows' troughs. "Too busy today," he mumbled.

Mandy frowned. She followed Grandpa around the barn while he finished his chores. Suddenly they both looked up as a strange sound filled the air.

"Come on," Grandpa called, racing out of the barn. Mandy raced out right behind him. Her boots splashed in the slush.

Grandpa pointed toward the sky. Mandy gasped at the sight. Hundreds of birds flew in a flock, honking loudly all the way. Mandy and Grandpa watched until the birds looked like thin black ribbons flowing in the distant sky.

"Canadian geese," Grandpa said. "They've come home for springtime."

"Where were they for the winter, Grandpa?" Mandy asked.

"They fly south where they can find food more easily," Grandpa said.

"How do they know the way?"

"It's built into their heads, like a gift," Grandpa said. "They know exactly where they belong, and they somehow manage to get there year after year."

"Mandy!" Mama called from the car. "Time to go to church."

" 'Bye, Grandpa."

Mandy told Mama about the geese. She thought about them all the way to church.

During the service Mandy heard the door open. She turned around. "Grandpa!" she whispered aloud.

Mama smiled. "Go ahead," she whispered softly. Mandy ran back to sit with Grandpa.

He winked when he saw her, and said, "Sometimes God's wild creatures are good teachers."

Suddenly Mandy understood. "You know where you belong, Grandpa, just like the geese."

Grandpa nodded and held Mandy's hand as they both looked out the window toward the sky.—V.L.K.

The Lord Corrects

Pay attention when the Lord corrects you. Heb. 12:5, TEV.

"Robbie," Mother said, "you know better than that. Don't make such slurpy noises when you eat."

"I don't see what difference it makes," Robbie said crossly. "The soup tastes good this way." He liked to slurp his soup. He looked at Grandpa and made a face.

"Makes a big difference," Grandpa said.

Robbie was surprised. Why would Grandpa say that? "Why?" Robbie asked. "Why does it make a difference?"

Grandpa smiled. "The Bible says that you should pay attention when the Lord corrects you. It says He corrects the people He loves."

Robbie frowned. "I don't understand. If God loves me, why doesn't He let me do what I want?"

"Because you'd be getting yourself in all kinds of trouble." He looked at Robbie with his 'now you listen' look. "God gave you your mom and dad to bring you up the right way, you know."

Robbie nodded. "But they're not God."

"No," Grandpa answered. "But good parents speak for God. So you'd best listen."

Robbie thought about what Grandpa had said. Grandpa knew a lot about the Bible and was probably right. Robbie looked at Mother. "OK," he said. "I think I understand. No more soup slurping."

Grandpa gave his shoulder a friendly squeeze. "That's my boy," he said. —N.C.P.

A Sad-Happy Story

In those days nothing and no one shall be hurt or destroyed in all my Holy Mountain, says the Lord. Isa. 65:25, TLB.

Tears ran down Heather's pink cheeks. "I don't think I'll ever be happy again," Heather sobbed. "Why did Boots die? He was such a good kitty."

Poor Boots. Sometime during the night he must have run in front of a car. Dad had found him in the road.

"Come here, sweetie," Mom called from the big chair by the fireplace. Heather snuggled in Mom's arms, and Mom held her tight while she cried.

"Do you know what, Heather? God's heart is hurting for you, too. Let me tell you a 'sad-happy' story. On this earth many sad things happen. Pets like your Boots die. A mama or a daddy might forget their love for each other and divorce. The leaders of one country get mad and fight another country. Satan brought sin into this world, and sin only brings sadness and hurt."

"But let me tell you a happy story. Before too long, Jesus will return to earth to take all who love Him home to heaven. In this new home wolves and lambs will eat together, snakes won't be poisonous, and no one will ever get sick or die."

"No kitty will get run over by a car?" Heather asked softly with a sniffle.

"That's right, Heather. Nothing will ever be hurt or destroyed in the new earth."

"Mom, I like that 'sad-happy' story," Heather said. "I sure hope Jesus comes soon."

(NOTE TO READERS: Talk about happy-sad times in your life and about Christ's soon return.)—P.M.M.

Mother and the Angel

Let the words of my mouth and the meditation of my heart be acceptable in Your sight, O Lord, my strength and my redeemer. Ps. 19:14. NKJV.

When my mother, Cora Barron, was a young girl, she and some of her friends were sitting in church one evening just before prayer meeting began. She happened to look around to the back of the church and saw a young man sitting alone. Her friends saw him too, and started giggling about the way he looked and the way he was dressed. The girls would look at him, whisper something to each other, and laugh.

My mother turned to her friends and said, "You shouldn't make fun of him like that. That's not nice." But the girls kept on laughing and talking about the man.

Once again my mother turned around to look at the man. This time the man raised his hand, pointed his finger at her, and said, "You will live a long time." Mother tells me that she turned quickly back toward the front of the church, then quickly turned to look at him again. He was gone.

The girls wondered who the man was and where he had gone. But my mother believes that God sent one of His angels to the church that night. For what reason, she did not know.

It reminded her that we must be careful of the way we talk about people. Whatever we say, our words should be pleasing to Jesus. Jesus and the angels are always listening to what we say, and they are happy when we are kind.

(NOTE TO READERS: Talk about ways children can be kind.)—C.B.T.

Help Me

Whatever you want others to do for you, do so for them.
Matt. 7:12, NASB.

Marty tried and tried to put his puzzle together. But the pieces wouldn't fit. His baby brother, Ricky, in the playpen, waved his arms and cooed.

"You can't help me," Marty told him. "You're too little." Ricky began to fuss.

Mother came into the family room and picked up Ricky. She changed his diaper and patted his back. Then she put him back in the playpen.

"Will you help me with my puzzle?" Marty asked.

"I don't have time right now," Mother said. "I'm doing the laundry."

"After you do the laundry will you help me?" Marty asked.

"No. I have to finish cleaning the house and take care of Ricky. He's a fussy baby today," Mother said, and went back to the laundry room.

Marty stuck out his lip. He needed help. But Mommy was too busy. She had lots of work to do. Now he would never get his puzzle together.

Suddenly Marty had an idea. He picked up all of his toys off the floor and put them in the toy box. Baby Ricky started to fuss again, so Marty played peekaboo with him. Then standing on tiptoe, he reached into the playpen for the musical teddy bear. Marty wound it up and put the bear close to Ricky. The baby listened. Then he popped his thumb into his mouth. Soon he was fast asleep.

When Mother came, Marty put his finger to his lips and whispered, "Shhh." Mother carried Ricky to his room.

"You're a good helper," Mother said when she came back. "You put all your toys away and took care of Ricky." She sat down at his little table. "I think I have time to help you with your puzzle now."—M.H.D.

Nurse Christy

Then he [Jesus] went down to Nazareth. . . . But his mother treasured all these things in her heart. Luke 2:51, NIV.

Christy's mother had been sick for a long time. When she got better and Dad felt he could go back to work, he called his 5-year-old daughter into Mom's room. "Christy, dear, do you think you can help Mother? She can be up part of the time, but she shouldn't be doing all the little errands she usually does."

"Christy's a good nurse. She'll take care of me," Mother said.

Christy's eyes sparkled. She ran and got a clean apron, then made herself a kind of nurse's hat from a piece of white paper. "I'll take good care of Mother," she promised.

"If you have any trouble, be sure to call on our neighbor," Dad said. He hugged Christy and went off to work.

All morning Christy played nurse. She brought juice and water. She brought buttered bread, fixed the way Mom had shown her. And she told her mother, "I have a surprise, but it won't be ready until lunch."

Mom rested and they talked. Christy was learning to read, so she read from her Bible story book. Before they knew it, it was time for lunch. "Where's my surprise?" Mother asked.

Christy went to the refrigerator. "Oh, no!" she cried. "The jello is still all runny." She had made it with cool water instead of boiling water, and it hadn't set!

Mother didn't care. She drank the runny jello and said that even real nurses sometimes make mistakes and that she'd remember Christy's help.—C.L.R.

The "Garbage Girl"

And God saw all that he had made, and it was very good. Gen. 1:31, REB.

Katya looked at the trees, birds, and animals God had made and began to think about the earth.

When she went inside, Daddy and Mama were making dinner. Katya said, "I'll put those tin cans into the recycling bin."

"Thank you," Daddy said with a smile.

After dinner as her parents cleaned up, Katya said, "I'll put the apple juice bottle into the recycling bin."

"Thank you," said Mama.

Right before she went to bed, Katya took all the old papers and put them into the recycling bin too.

"Good girl," said Daddy.

Mama said, "Katya, I never knew you loved taking out garbage."

Katya smiled. "I hate taking out garbage," she said. "But I love the trees, birds, and animals. And I especially love the earth!"

Does your town have recycling bins? Does your family recycle? — V.L.K.

Fill Your Mind With Good

Fill your minds with those things that are good and that deserve praise. Phil. 4:8, TEV.

"But I want to see that scary program," Jerry cried. "Everyone at school's going to watch it."

Dad frowned. "Jerry, we don't do things just because other people do."

Mother nodded. "And *everyone* can't be doing it— because *we* aren't. And the Castles aren't. And the Raymonds aren't."

Jerry frowned. "I still don't see why I can't watch it. It's just one show."

Mother sighed. "One show leads to another, just like one bad deed leads to another. God doesn't want us to watch such things."

Jerry shook his head. "But Bob's big brother says the Bible can't tell us not to watch them. He says there weren't any TV shows when the Bible was written."

"That's right," Dad said. "There weren't. But God plainly told His people to pay attention to what was good, to think about being the kind who show that they are God's people. God's people are supposed to be doing good things, not watching shows about bad things."

Jerry thought hard. He'd heard the Sabbath school teacher say that looking at bad things *could* make a person want to do them.

He looked at Mother and Dad. "All right," he said. "I belong to God."—N.C.P.

The Snowflake

Thank you for making me so wonderfully complex! It is amazing to think about. Your workmanship is marvelous. Ps. 139:14, TLB.

"Mom, look at the snowflakes. Aren't they beautiful?" Maria called as she pressed her little brown nose against the picture window of their second-floor apartment. She had never lived where it snowed before.

All day long the snowflakes fell steadily over the big city, covering the gray of the sidewalks below. Snowplows rumbled through the streets, making piles of snow along the curbs. By the next morning the sun was shining brightly over the blanket of sparkling white.

"Put your warmest clothes on, Maria," Mama called to her daughter. "Uncle Roberto will be here shortly to take you and your cousins to the park."

For the next several hours the kids played in the snow. They built a snowman, took turns sledding down the hill, and then finished off with a friendly snowball fight. All that fun because of the millions of little snowflakes that had gently fallen the day before.

A snowflake is an amazing thing. No snowflake is exactly alike. One might have a pine-needle design around its edges. Another may be star-shaped. Another may have a chicken-feet pattern. But every snowflake is beautiful and special in its own way.

You too are an amazing creation! No one has been made quite like you. Some children may be tall, some short. Some children have brown skin. Others are pale with freckles. Some have red hair, others black. Aren't you glad we don't all look alike? The next time you see a snowflake, remember that God has made you beautiful and special in your very own way.—P.M.M.

Baseball or Books?

Children, obey your parents in all things, for this is well pleasing to the Lord. Col. 3:20, NKJV.

"Mother," shouted Allen as he ran into the house from school and laid his books on the table, "all the boys are going to the park to play baseball. May I go play with them?"

"Allen, you know the rules of the house," said Mother. "Homework first; then you may go out and play."

"But I'll never get out to play with all this homework I have to do," grumbled Allen. Mother told Allen that if he'd stop fussing and do his homework, perhaps there'd be time for him to play baseball. But his homework had to be finished first.

Allen was mad. He wanted to play baseball. Instead of going to his bedroom to study, Allen took his books from the table and went downstairs to the basement. He sat on the floor with his books opened. But Allen's mind was not on schoolwork. It was on the baseball game at the park.

Allen took his history book and tried to read a story for tomorrow's class. It was hard for him to read about something that took place a long time ago when there was a good baseball game going on right now.

Baseball. Allen stood up and walked to a small window that opened out under the porch and led to the street. Baseball was all that was on Allen's mind as he climbed out the window, crawled under the porch, and came out to the street. He ran to the park and soon was playing baseball with the other boys.

Father came home early from work that day and asked Mother where Allen was. Mother said that Allen was down in the basement doing his homework. Father went down to the basement to speak with Allen, but all he saw were Allen's books. Then Father saw the open window and knew Allen had sneaked out through it. Father closed and locked the window, then went upstairs to tell Mother what had happened. He sat down to wait for Allen to come back from the park.

It was starting to get dark. Allen ran as fast as he could down the street toward home from the park. When he got to his house, he crawled under the porch, got to the window—and found it locked! So Allen crawled back out from under the porch and walked around the house to the back door. He quietly opened the back door and walked into the kitchen. There sat Mother and Father. They'd been waiting for Allen to come home.

Allen had disobeyed Mother and Father, but even more Allen had disobeyed Jesus. He knew Mother hadn't seen him sneak out of the window, but Jesus had seen him, and that had made Jesus very sad. Mother and Father told Allen that Jesus sees everything that he does and that it is better to obey and be happy. Allen promised he would obey and not go out without permission.—C.B.T.

Terry

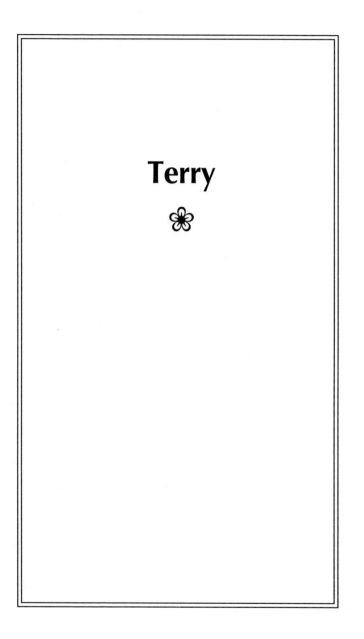

Terry Moves to the City

I am with you, and I will protect you everywhere you go. Gen. 28:15, ICB.

Today was a very busy day for me and my family. We got up early in the morning, packed our suitcases, put our furniture in a big truck, and moved to a new home in the city.

I miss my country house. I miss hearing the birds singing outside my bedroom window. I miss seeing the white, fluffy clouds above the cornfields and the pretty flowers in the meadows.

But most of all I miss my best friend, Beverly, who lived just down the road from me. We used to play together every day in the cool shade of the oak tree in my front yard.

My new room in the city apartment building has a little window that looks down on a busy street. I hear roaring engines, honking horns, and lots of footsteps. I didn't hear one bird singing all afternoon. I heard only strange, new sounds. It made me a little afraid.

After supper we had worship sitting on boxes and piles of clothes. We sang one of my favorite Sabbath school songs, then my daddy read a verse from the Bible. This is what it said: " 'I am with you, and I will protect you everywhere you go.' "

It made me happy to know Jesus moved with us from the country to the city. And as I close my eyes to sleep I feel a little better because, even in my little room above the noisy street, Jesus is still watching over me.—C.M.

Terry Is Afraid

Don't be afraid, because I am your God. Isa. 41:10, ICB.

Rrrrrr. Rrrrrrr-blam. Bang. What is that awful noise?
Tat-tat-tat. Screeeech. Crunch! I open my eyes and look around. Where am I?

Rrrrrrr. Ding-ding-ding. Blam! I sit up and call as loudly as I can, "Mommy! Daddy! Come quick!"

Daddy appears at my bedroom door, his electric razor buzzing in his hand. "What's the matter, Terry?" he asks.

Mommy squeezes past and runs to my bedside. "What's the matter?" she asks, putting her arms around me. "Did something frighten you?"

Clank. Clank. Crunch, crunch. Bang!

Mommy and Daddy smile at each other. Then they lift me up and carry me to the window. "Is that what frightened you?" they ask.

I look down on the street and see a strange truck with strong men running around carrying big metal cans and plastic bags. "Don't be afraid," my daddy says. "That's just the city garbage truck picking up the trash."

Rrrrrr. Rrrrrrrr. The funny-looking truck roars down the street and turns the corner. I begin to cry. "I miss my home in the country," I say. "I miss Beverly, and the big tree, and I miss hearing the birds sing to me."

Daddy holds me tightly in his arms. "I know," he says softly. "I miss those things too. That's why I'm going to bring home a big surprise today after I start my new job. Would you like that?"

"Oh, yes," I nod. "I love surprises!"

Can you think of a happy surprise you had one time?— C.M.

A New Friend

If we love each other, God lives in us. 1 John 4:11, ICB.

"Hello," a voice calls to me from the end of the long hallway outside my apartment door. "What's your name?" it asks.

"My name's Terry," I say. "What's your name?"

"Nathan. My mom calls me Nat. You can call me Nat if you want to."

I see a boy with a red sweater walking toward me. "Do you want to play video games?" he asks. "I've got a bunch of toys in my room. We can play rocketship or airplane pilot or anything."

He kicks at a pretend ball and I catch it. "We could play football, too, if you want," he adds.

"I have to ask my mom first," I tell him.

We walk together into my apartment. "Your house is a mess," he says.

"I know," I laugh. We find Mom in my bedroom hanging some yellow curtains. "Can I go play with Nat?" I ask her.

Mom looks down from her ladder. "Hello," she says with a smile. "Are you Mrs. Fredrick's son?"

"Yes, ma'am," Nat answers. "My mom's working at her computer and my dad doesn't live at our house anymore, so I don't have anybody to play with."

"I know," Mom says quietly. "I talked to your mother this morning. I'll be happy for you and Terry to play together. Just don't make too much noise, OK?"

"OK," we say. As we walk down the hallway I smile to myself. Maybe Nat can be my new best friend in the city.

(NOTE TO READERS: Talk about what makes a good new friend.)—C.M.

Be a Missionary at Home

[Jesus has] put gladness in my heart. Ps. 4:7, KJV.

It's lunchtime. I sit down with my mom to eat a sandwich. "You know," I say while eating a piece of bread with lettuce on it, "Nat has lots of toys, but he's sad. Why is that?"

My mommy pours me a glass of milk. "I think he misses his daddy. How would you feel, Terry, if your daddy went away?"

"I'd feel very, very sad," I say, wiping my mouth with a napkin.

"Even if you had lots of toys?" Mommy asks.

I think for a minute. "Yes. I love Daddy more than all the toys in the whole world."

"And that's the way Jesus wants us to love Him, too," Mommy tells me. "He wants to be more important to us than anything."

"Why?" I ask.

Mommy sits down beside me. "Because loving Jesus is the only way for people to find happiness. Remember the text Daddy read this morning for worship? It said, '[Jesus has] put gladness in my heart.' That's what He does when we love Him most."

"Then I'd better tell Nat to love Jesus so he can be happy again," I say thoughtfully.

Mommy nods. "Good idea. Everyone needs to hear about Jesus."

"Everyone?" I gasp. "How can I tell all the people in this big city that Jesus wants to give them happiness?"

"You can begin by telling Nat. And I'll tell his mom, too. We'll be missionaries right here in our apartment building, OK?"

"OK!" I say with a smile. —C.M.

A Surprise for Terry

The Lord gives me strength and makes me sing. Ex. 15:2, ICB.

I sit by my window looking down at the noisy street below. Everyone seems to be in such a hurry. The cars, buses, the businesspeople scurry here and there like busy ants. I sigh. Evening is different in the country. When the sun begins to set in the country, the cows walk slowly toward the barn, and the ducks take one more flight around the pond, then settle in for the night.

Even the songbirds sing softer as the big sun sets. But here in the city I can't hear any birds singing.

"Tweet." What was that? "Tweet, tweet."

I scratch my head. "It sounds like a bird," I say to myself. "But I don't see any birds outside."

"Tweet, tweet, trillll." There it is again.

I look toward my bedroom door. My daddy is standing there with a little cage in his hand. In the cage I see something moving. "Hi, Terry," Daddy says.

"Tweet, tweet, trillll." Then I know what it is. "Daddy!" I shout. "You brought me a bird for my very own. Listen. Listen to it sing!"

"Tweetel, tweetel, chirp, chirp, chirp." The little bird's happy song makes me laugh and laugh. "This is a wonderful surprise," I say, giving my daddy a big hug. "Now I can have pretty bird songs in my bedroom again, just like in our country home."

Daddy smiles. Mommy smiles. And I smile. The bird just sings and sings.—C.M.

What Terry Learned

Be of good courage, and [God] shall strengthen your heart. Ps. 31:24, KJV.

My first day in the city has been fun. I saw a strange-looking truck take away the trash, found a new friend named Nat, decided to be a missionary right in my apartment building, and got a little bird to sing to me.

Now we're sitting down for family worship. The supper dishes have been washed and dried, and I listen to Daddy tell Mommy all about his new job. I'm wearing my pajamas—the ones with the duck on the front.

Daddy says to me, "Well, Terry, what did you learn today?"

I think and think. Then I say, "I learned that if you're sad and afraid, just wait a little bit and things will get better."

"Very good," Daddy says. "And how about you, Mommy? What did you learn today?"

Mommy thinks and thinks. Then she says, "I learned that there are many people in the city who need to know that Jesus loves them."

"Oh, yes," I say. "I learned that too."

Daddy smiles. He opens his Bible and finds a special verse. "Listen to this," he says. " 'Be of good courage, and [God] shall strengthen your heart.' "

Then Daddy says, "Today I learned that no matter what you want to do for Jesus, He will help you."

Together we kneel down and pray, thanking Jesus for His love.

Mommy, Daddy, and I agree that it's been a very interesting day.

(NOTE TO READERS: Talk about what you learned today.)—C.M.

A Witness for Jesus

You will be his witness to all people. Acts 22:15, ICB.

Beep. Beep. Our taxi bumps down the street as we ride to the grocery story. Beep, beep, it says to the other cars.

Mommy looks out the window and watches the people and trucks and buildings pass by. I watch too.

At a corner I see a boy standing with his daddy, waiting for the light to turn green. "Hello," I call out. The boy looks up at me and waves. Then we hurry away.

"There sure isn't much time to talk to other people in the city," I say with a sigh. "Everyone is moving around all the time."

"That's right, Terry," Mommy says. "The city is a very busy place."

"Then how am I supposed to tell people about Jesus if I can't talk to them?" I want to know.

Mommy looks down at me. "You are telling them about Jesus."

"How?" I ask. "All I do is smile and wave."

"That's right," Mommy says. "By being friendly and smiling, you're showing God's love to people."

"I am?" I gasp. "Just by smiling and being friendly I'm showing people God's love?"

"Absolutely," Mommy says nodding her head. "Jesus wants us to be kind and loving to others. He wants us to smile and wave, and help people every chance we get."

"I like showing people God's love with my smile," I say. As the taxi bounces down the street, I smile and wave at everybody I see.—C.M.

A Smile for Terry's Face

Happy are the people whose God is the Lord. Ps. 144:15, ICB.

The grocery store is filled with fruits, vegetables, cereals, soups, bread, milk, and even a few toys. I like toys.

Mommy pushes the cart down the isle and places brightly colored boxes into it. The boxes have pictures of food on them.

"I know why there are pictures on these boxes," I say. "That's so you'll know what's inside."

Mommy nods her head. "That's right, Terry. By looking at the picture, I know what I'm buying."

I watch Mommy put boxes of macaroni, beans, and cereal into her cart. Then I have an idea.

"Mommy," I say, "you told me that Jesus wants to live in my heart. Well, I'd better keep a smile on my face so people will know He's there. It's like a picture on a box. When people see my smile, they know Jesus is inside."

Mommy stops pushing her cart and lifts me up into her arms. "That's a wonderful idea," she says. "I'll smile too. Then people will know Jesus is in my heart. That way we can be missionaries everywhere we go!"

I feel happy inside. "Hey, Mommy," I say, "can we be missionaries over there where the toys are?"—C.M.

Terry Helps a Street Person

Anything you did for any of my people here, you also did for me. Matt. 25:40, ICB.

"Look, Mommy," I say as we're riding in the taxi. "Why is that lady pushing a shopping cart down the sidewalk? Is she going to buy some groceries for her family?"

Mommy shakes her head. "No, Terry, she's not buying groceries. They call someone like her a street person, and the shopping cart is her home."

"What do you mean?" I ask.

Mommy sighs a sad sigh. "There are many people in the city who have no home, no family, no money to buy groceries. They just live outside on the streets and sidewalks. Sometimes other people help them by giving them food to eat and a place to sleep, but most of the time street people have to search for food and shelter."

I look up at my mommy. "It makes me want to cry," I say softly.

"Me too," Mommy nods. Then she places her hand on my shoulder. "Would you like to help that street person?"

"How?" I want to know.

Mommy reaches into our grocery sack and pulls out a bag of apples. Then she asks the taxi driver to stop. I watch as she walks over to the lady pushing the shopping cart. "Here," she says, "my son and I would like you to have these apples. And we'll pray for you every day."

The lady with the cart takes the apples and smiles. "Thank you," she says. Then she pushes her cart down the sidewalk and disappears in the crowd of people passing by.—C.M.

Terry Thanks Jesus

Thank the Lord because he is good. His love continues forever. 1 Chron. 6:34, ICB.

"Tweet. Tweet. Trilll." My little bird sits in his cage and sings a good morning song to me.

I open my eyes and see the sunlight coming through the window.

Turning, I lie and listen to my bird and think about our old house in the country.

Mommy calls from the kitchen, "Terry. Terry? Are you awake?"

"Yes," I answer sleepily.

Mommy appears at the door. "Get dressed and come for breakfast. I made your favorite—toast with strawberries on it."

As I wash my face and put on my shirt, I think about the street lady we saw yesterday. Was she going to have a delicious breakfast this morning?

Sitting down to eat, I look at all the food my mommy has fixed. There's milk, cereal, toast, nuts, and a bowl of oranges.

"Would you like to pray?" Mommy asks.

I fold my hands and close my eyes. "Dear Jesus . . ." I stop because I think about the street lady again. "Dear Jesus . . ." My mommy puts her hand on my head. I feel a tear run down my cheek. "Dear Jesus, thank You for my breakfast. Thank You for my room and my bird, and my mommy, and my daddy. Thank You for everything. Amen."

Then I smile, because I know Jesus loves me very much.— C.M.

Terry Visits Daddy at Work

My Father never stops working. And so I work, too. John 5:17, ICB.

The elevator goes up, up, up. Sometimes we stop and people get on. Sometimes we stop and people get off. But my mommy and I stay on the elevator and go higher and higher.

Finally Mommy says, "Here's our floor."

The door opens, and we step out into a pretty room with big desks and lots of busy people walking around. A lady sitting next to the elevator looks up and smiles. "Hello," she says. "May I help you?"

I walk over to her and say, "Yes. My name is Terry and we came to see my daddy. Do you know where he is?"

The lady smiles. "What does your daddy do?" she asks.

I scratch my head and think and think. What does he do? He gets up in the morning, shaves his chin, eats breakfast, kisses Mommy and makes her laugh, then goes to work.

When we lived in our country home, I could see what he did just by watching him. He didn't go far away. He didn't ride in an elevator. He just went to the barn or the fields.

"Mommy," I ask, "does Daddy work even when I can't see him?"

"Yes, he does," Mommy says. "Both Daddy and Jesus take good care of us even though we can't see where they work. Isn't that nice?"

I nod my head. I like having my daddy and Jesus take good care of me, even if I can't see them working.—C.M.

A Picture in Daddy's Office

So we have been sent to speak for Christ. 2 Cor. 5:20, ICB.

Mommy looks at the lady sitting beside the elevator and says, "My husband fixes things—you know, machines, electric wiring."

"Oh," the lady says with a big smile. "You must mean Mr. Williams, our new maintenance director. He's a very nice man. He's always kind and helpful. His office is over there."

Mommy takes me by the hand and leads me around the desks and through the busy crowd of people. We pass a machine making copies of a letter, and go around another machine that's making funny noises as a lady presses keys on it. And we walk beside a ringing telephone.

Then we come to an office door. Mommy points to some letters on a sign hanging next to it. "Look, Terry, that's your daddy's name," she says proudly. "This is where he works."

When Daddy sees me, he picks me up and gives me a big kiss. Then he gives Mommy a hug. "Thank you for coming to visit me," he says.

I look around my daddy's office. I see a picture of Jesus hanging by the window. I point to it and say, "I like that picture."

Daddy nods. "I like it too. I want everyone to know that I love Jesus. That's why I put it there."

I look at Mommy and begin to laugh. "I think Daddy wants to be a missionary too, just like you and I do," I say.

Mommy nods. "I guess we're a missionary family. I'm sure that makes Jesus very happy."—C.M.

Angels in the City

He has put his angels in charge of you. They will watch over you wherever you go. Ps. 91:11, ICB.

My daddy's office is high above the city. From his window I can see many other tall buildings reaching up toward the blue sky.

Far below, I can see little cars and people moving along the streets and sidewalks. The city is a very busy and crowded place even when you look at it from way up high.

"Daddy," I ask, "can Jesus see everybody down there? There are so many people and they're so busy. How can He help them all?"

"There are a lot of people down on the streets, aren't there, Terry?" he agrees, looking at the streets far below us. "That's why Jesus gives everyone an angel. Angels help Jesus take care of the people He loves."

"Jesus gives everyone an angel?" I ask.

"That's right. You, me, Mommy, and all those people down there have angels right by their sides."

I look at the streets and buildings. Then I shake my head. "The city sure has a lot of angels in it! Everyone should feel very safe."

Daddy looks a little sad. "Some people don't want Jesus or His angels to help them. They want to do everything all by themselves. That's why so many people are sad. Satan makes troubles come, and then those people have no one to help them."

I press my face against the window and think about how sad it must be not to know about Jesus and His angels. "I will always remember my angel is beside me," I say softly.—C.M.

Lunch in a Restaurant

Look, I have given you all the plants that have grain for seeds. And I have given you all the trees whose fruits have seeds in them. They will be food for you. Gen. 1:29, ICB.

It's lunchtime, and my mommy and daddy take me to a restaurant to eat. I study the pictures on the menu. Everything looks delicious.

My stomach growls and growls, as though it's saying "Feed me!"

"I think I'll have some of this," I say, pointing to a pretty picture.

Mom looks at my choice. "I don't think you want any of that," she says. "It may look good, Terry, but it's not healthy. Your body should have only good things in it."

"How do I know what food is good and what food isn't?" I ask.

Daddy leans toward me. "Good food has good things in it, like vegetables, fruits, grains, nuts. Some of the food on this menu has other things in it. If you eat those foods, you might get sick."

"But the picture looks so nice," I say with a sigh. "How am I supposed to know what food to eat?"

"Just find out what's inside," Mommy says. "Then choose only foods that Jesus made for us to eat. There's a verse in the Bible that says, 'Look, I have given you all the plants that have grain for seeds. And I have given you all the trees whose fruits have seeds in them. They will be food for you.' " Mommy gave me a big smile. "Jesus wants us to enjoy the natural foods He made for us. Then we can be healthy."—C.M.

Jesus in Your Heart

A good person has good things in his heart. And so he speaks the good things that come from his heart. Matt. 12:35, ICB.

After lunch we go back to Daddy's office. He has to work, so we say goodbye. As we're riding down in the elevator, I think about the picture of Jesus in Daddy's office. Then I begin to worry.

"Mommy," I say, "what if some people don't go into Daddy's office. They won't see the picture of Jesus, and they'll never know that Daddy loves Him."

Mommy looks down at me. "Then Daddy has to show them Jesus another way," she says.

"How?" I want to know.

Mommy presses her hand against my chest. "Terry, if Jesus lives in here, then people will know you love Him by what you do with your hands and your mouth and your feet.

"Your hands will work hard helping people. Your mouth will speak kindly and honestly, and your feet will take you only to the places where Jesus would want you to go."

"I understand," I say. "It's like we are pictures of Jesus. When people look at us, they know Jesus lives in our hearts. Right?"

"That's right," Mom agrees. "The Bible says, 'A good person has good things in his heart. And so he speaks the good things that come from his heart.' "

"I'm going to put a picture of Jesus on my face, too," I say as the elevator door opens. And as Mommy and I walk out to the taxi, I smile and smile.—C.M.

Nat Learns About Heaven

I will come back. Then I will take you to be with me. John 14:3, ICB.

Nat and I sit on the steps of our apartment building watching people pass by. Mommy sits beside us reading a book.

Suddenly Nat points to a big black car coming around the corner.

"Look, Terry," he calls out. "Here comes a policeman!"

I watch the shiny car drive slowly past our building. The man in the driver's seat waves at us. Nat and I wave back.

"Mommy," I say, "is that policeman looking for burglars?"

"Maybe," she says. "Or he might be just checking to make sure everything's all right on this street. Policemen work hard to keep us safe in the city."

Nat sighs. "Wouldn't it be nice if there was a city where no one stole things and where policemen could just play baseball all day?"

Mommy nods. "There is a city like that."

"Where?" Nat wants to know.

"It's called 'heaven.' Jesus lives there. Someday we can live there too, if we choose to love and obey God. There won't be any burglars in heaven. And there won't be any drugs or guns or knives." Mommy ruffles Nat's hair. "In fact, policemen won't even have a job in heaven, because there won't be any reason to worry about us. We'll be safe and sound with Jesus."

"Can we all move to that city?" Nat asks.

"Yes, when Jesus comes to take us there," Mommy says. "It will be a wonderful place to live. Children can play and play without ever being afraid. And both kids and grown-ups can learn exciting things about nature if they want to."

Nat thinks for a moment. "Will Jesus play baseball with me?"

Mommy smiles. "He'll be happy to, I'm sure."—C.M.

Picnic in the Park

Let the fields and everything in them show their joy. Then all the trees of the forest will sing for joy. Ps. 96:12, ICB.

"Watch how high I can go," I shout as I swing back and forth above the soft green grass. "Are you watching?"

My mommy and daddy look up from the picnic blanket where they are getting food out of a big brown basket.

I pump my feet forward and backward and go higher and higher.

"Wheeee!" I call. "Wheeeeee!"

As I swish through the air in the swing, I look around at the trees and bushes spreading across the city park. The sunshine feels warm on my face.

"Hey, Terry," Mommy calls. "Your picnic dinner is ready."

I let my feet drag on the ground and stop the swing. Then I run over to the blanket and plop down. "You know," I say with a sigh, "this city nature is almost like country nature."

"It's the very same," Daddy says. "God shows city people how much He loves them with flowers, grasses, and trees just like He shows country folk how much He loves them. Isn't it nice that God shows everyone His beautiful nature? And we should always remember to keep His nature clean. That's why we pick up all our picnic papers and place them in the big trash can when we're finished."

As we bow our heads to pray, I say, "Dear Jesus, thank You for this delicious food. And thank You for Your beautiful nature. We'll take good care of it for You. Amen."—C.M.

Where Is Heaven?

I am going [to heaven] to prepare a place for you. John 14:2, ICB.

Soft, fluffy clouds drift high in the sky above our heads. Mommy, Daddy, and I lie on our backs, watching them move like big, white boats sailing on a smooth blue ocean. In the distance I can hear cars and trucks speeding along the highway that passes close to the city park. Our picnic is finished, and our tummies feel full and happy. I turn to face my mommy. "God lives in heaven, right?" I ask.

"Yes, that's right," she says.

"But where is heaven? Is it far from here?"

Daddy points toward the sky. "It's waaaay up there somewhere, Terry. It's beyond the clouds, beyond the stars."

"Can we get there in an airplane?" I ask. "Or how about the space shuttle? Can the space shuttle go there?"

"No," Mommy says, "only angels and Jesus can go there right now. But someday we'll all go there together. Jesus will take us."

I think for a minute. "But where in heaven will we live? Do we have a house there?"

Daddy smiles. The Bible says our house is being built right now. Jesus said, "I am going [to heaven] to prepare a place for you."

"Really?" I say. "Jesus is building a house for us to live in?"

"That's right," Mommy says. "A big, beautiful house just for us."—C.M.

A Package From Jesus

I love you . . . with a love that will last forever. I became your friend because of my love and kindness. Jer. 31:3, ICB.

Tap, tap, tap. Someone is at our apartment door. *Tap, tap, tap.* Mommy goes to see who it is.

"Oh, hello, Mr. Collins," I hear her say. Mr. Collins is our postman. He brings mail to our apartment building everyday.

"I have a package for Terry Williams," the postman says. I look up from my picture book. Did he say he had a package for me?

Mommy comes into my room. "Look," she says with a big smile on her face. "Grandma sent a package just for you."

I jump up and run to my desk. "Let's open it," I shout happily. Quickly I unwrap the package and look inside. There I see some animal books, a pretty T-shirt, and a puzzle. "Wow!" I cry. "Look at all this neat stuff Grandma sent me!"

At worship that night I show Daddy all my new things. I tell him that I've never had anyone send me a package before. He shakes his head. "Yes, you have," he says. "Jesus sends you a package of letters every day, and He wants me to read them to you."

"He does?" I gasp. "What did Jesus send me today?"

Daddy opens his big Bible and reads. " 'I love you . . . with a love that will last forever. I became your friend because of my love and kindness.' "

"See," Daddy says, "this is a love letter to you from Jesus. The Bible is a big package of love letters sent just for us."—C.M.

Living Forever

The grass dies, and the flowers fall. But the word of our God will live forever. Isa. 40:8, ICB.

"Oh dear." Mommy looks at the plant sitting on the window ledge. "My beautiful flowers have died. I guess my plant didn't get enough sunlight or fresh air. Too bad."

Mommy dumps the wilted plant into the garbage pail and sighs, "It's not easy growing flowers in a little apartment in a big city."

I look down at the poor dead plant. "Why do things have to die?" I ask sadly. "Even people and animals die. That's what happened to Grandpa, remember?"

Mommy sits down and pulls me on her lap. "Yes, Terry, I remember," she says. "Things die because Satan makes them die. But Jesus has promised that someday death and Satan will be destroyed and everyone who loves God will live forever. If Jesus made that promise, you can believe it."

"Then I can see Grandpa again?" I ask.

"Yes, and you'll meet your aunt Carol and your cousin John. There's a verse in the Bible that says, 'The grass dies, and the flowers fall. But the word of our God will live forever.' Satan cannot destroy Jesus, and Jesus has promised us in His word that we'll live forever with Him in heaven."

I look down at the dead plant. I'm glad Jesus has promised to stop death. I want flowers, and grandpas, to live forever.

(Talk about loss; a pet, friend, or family member who died.)—C.M.

Terry Pleases Jesus

Children, obey your parents in all things. This pleases the Lord. Col. 3:20, ICB.

"Terry?" my daddy's voice calls from the kitchen. "Would you please come here and help me?"

I put my car in its pretend garage and run to the kitchen. "What do you want me to do?" I ask.

"I have to take the garbage out to the dumpster. Will you carry this bag for me?"

I lift the bag into my arms and follow Daddy down the apartment steps and behind the building. We place our plastic bags of garbage inside the big metal trash bin and then head back up the stairs.

"Do you know what?" Daddy asks as he opens the door for me. "Jesus likes it when children obey their parents. The Bible says it *pleases* Him."

"It does?" I ask. "Does Jesus know when I obey you?"

"Yes. He looks after all His children, grown up and small. And he likes to see us doing what our parents, or our boss, or our teachers tell us to do."

"I'll remember that," I say. "When I obey Mommy and Daddy, I'm pleasing Jesus. That makes everyone happy."—C.M.

Doing Something to Help

Happy is the person who thinks about the poor. Ps. 41:1, ICB.

I scratch my head and frown. "Daddy," I say, "read that text again."

Daddy looks down at his Bible and reads. " 'Happy is the person who thinks about the poor.' "

"I don't understand," I say. "When I think about the homeless lady and about Mr. McFarland who lives above us, it doesn't make me happy. They are both poor. When I think about them, I feel sad."

Daddy nods thoughtfully. "You're right, Terry. But Jesus didn't mean for us to only *think* about them. We're supposed to think and then *do* something. That's what Jesus did when He was here on earth."

"Well," I say, "I think about Mr. McFarland a lot because I see him every day. His coat is torn and his shoes have big holes in them. What can I *do* to help him?"

Daddy takes me by the hand and we go to his closet. "I don't need two coats to wear," he says, "and one pair of good shoes should do me fine. Let's take this extra coat and these nice shiny shoes up to Mr. McFarland's apartment and ask him if he'd like to use them."

"Oh, that's a good idea," I say, clapping my hands. "Then when we think about Mr. McFarland, we can be happy, because we *did* something."—C.M.

Do Not Follow Bad People

My child, sinners will try to lead you into sin. But do not follow them. Prov. 1:10, ICB.

"What are those men doing?" I ask as Mommy and I walk along the sidewalk outside our apartment building.

A man runs to a car and shows something to the driver. Then the driver gives him some money and the man goes away. Mommy holds my hand tightly.

"Terry," Mommy whispers, "the man is selling pills that make the man's body weak."

"Why did that man in the car buy them?"

"Because those pills are drugs that make him feel good for a while. When the good feeling stops, the man buys more drugs to feel good again. Every time he uses those drugs his body grows weaker. The driver is a drug addict. The man is a drug dealer."

I think for a minute. "Does Jesus love the drug dealer?"

"Oh, yes," Mommy says. "Jesus loves him very much. And we must too. But the drug dealer doesn't love Jesus. That's why he's doing a bad thing. The Bible says a person is a *sinner* when he or she doesn't obey Jesus.

"But Jesus wants to forgive him, just as He wants to forgive us when we do bad things."

I watch the drug dealer walk around the corner and disappear. Maybe someday, when I'm older, I can tell him that Jesus loves him and wants him to do only good things.—C.M.

Terry and Nat Go to the Zoo

So God made the wild animals, the tame animals and all the small crawling animals. Gen. 1:25, ICB.

"Look at those big ears!" Nat and I watch the elephant moving back and forth in his cage. "He can probably hear us whisper a mile away."

Daddy and Mommy giggle. "So we'd better watch what we say around here," Mommy says.

Nat throws a peanut to the elephant. The big animal scoops it up with his long nose and plops it into his mouth.

"I like this zoo," I say as we head for the monkey island. "God sure made some funny-looking animals."

Nat looks at me in surprise. "God made all these animals?" he asks. "Even that hippopotamus?"

"That's what the Bible says," Daddy answers. "It also tells us that God made a special animal to be His friend forever. Do you know what that animal is?"

"A dog?" Nat asks. "Dogs are good friends. A cow? A horse?"

Daddy shakes his head no.

"What animal did God make to be His special friend?" Nat asks.

"I know. I know!" I call, jumping up and down almost like a monkey. "God made people to be His friends."

"That's right, Terry," Daddy says with a smile. "And I think we're much better looking than hippopotamuses. Don't you agree?"

Nat laughs and laughs. I laugh and laugh. Mommy and Daddy laugh and laugh. And the hippopotamus dives under the water and swims away. —C.M.

Some of God's Helpers

"I will bring back your health. And I will heal your injuries," says the Lord. Jer. 30:17, ICB.

"Listen," I say to my mommy and daddy while we're eating breakfast. "Do you hear that siren?"

They listen carefully. "Yes, Terry, we hear it."

I run to the window and watch as an ambulance comes down our street and hurries past, its lights flashing and its siren wailing. Somebody somewhere is sick or hurt. The ambulance turns a corner. Then everything is quiet again.

At morning worship Daddy picks up his big Bible. He reads, "I will bring back your health. And I will heal your injuries."

"Daddy," I say, "how can God help us when we're sick? He's so far away in heaven."

Daddy nods his head. "It does seem impossible, but He has helpers here on earth."

"He does?" I ask. "Who helps God make us well?" Then I remember the ambulance. "Wait, I know. The doctors and nurses and the people driving the ambulance are His helpers, right?"

"That's right," Daddy says. "God can send someone to our bedside to help us. Or we can go to the hospital or clinic when we're sick or injured. It makes me feel good to know God is so close by when I need Him. When we pray for help, He comes running. When we hear a siren, we can know God's helpers are on their way!"—C.M.

God's Love Is Better Than Being Rich

It will be very hard for rich people to enter the kingdom of God! Luke 18:24, ICB.

"Look at that big car," I say as we drive along one of the streets in our city. "Why are the windows all dark?"

Daddy looks at the big car as it speeds by. "That's a rich person's automobile. Rich people like to have privacy while they sit on the back seat and let their driver take them where they want to go."

I think for a minute. "This morning you read a Bible verse that says it's hard for rich people to go to God's kingdom. Are all rich people bad?"

"Oh no, Terry," Daddy says. "Most rich people are good and honest. They work hard for their money. But Jesus knows that when you have lots of money, it's easy to forget about Him. You might stop depending on Him to help you. You might stop asking Him for His blessings. Then Satan works hard to make you forget God completely."

The big car turns a corner and stops in front of a tall building. A man with white gloves runs to the car door and opens it. Some people get out. They're wearing beautiful suits and pretty dresses. As we drive by, I watch them go into the building.

"Being rich would be nice," I tell Mommy and Daddy, "but I don't want to forget about God and how much He helps me."

"Good," Daddy says with a smile. "Having lots of money is nice. But remembering God's love is much, much better."—C.M.

Terry and Nat Go to Church

The seventh day is the sabbath of the Lord thy God. Ex. 20:10, KJV.

It's Sabbath morning, and I'm getting ready to go to church with my mommy and daddy. Last night I asked Nat if he wanted to go, and he said yes.

We drive in the car for a little while, then park in a parking lot. My city church is big. My Sabbath school class is big. The organ is big. The seats are big. Even the bathroom is big.

Nat looks at all the people walking around in my church. He listens to the songs, watches my teacher tell a story with felts, hears two people play on their trumpets, and walks up with me for the children's story. We have lots of fun.

When we're in the car going back home, Nat says, "Terry, I've never been to church on Saturday. Why don't you go to church on Sunday like the other people in our building?"

Mommy smiles and says, "We go to church on Saturday because Jesus wants us to. He told us to remember to keep

His seventh day holy. The seventh day is Saturday. We call it 'the Sabbath.' Jesus is happy when we worship Him on other days, but the seventh day is very special. He blessed it and made it holy."

"Well, I like the songs and the stories," Nat says. "Going to your church was fun. Can I go with you again?"

"Sure," Daddy nods. "You can come every week if your mom says it's OK."

Nat smiles. I smile. And I think Jesus is smiling too.—C.M.

Terry Visits the Planetarium

When you look up at the sky, you see the sun, moon and stars. The Lord your God has made these things for all people everywhere. Deut. 4:19, ICB.

"What is this place?" I ask as Daddy, Nat, and I sit down in a dark, round room. In the middle of the room is a big funny-looking machine.

Daddy leans back and says, "It's called a planetarium. We're going to see the night sky in a few minutes."

"But," Nat says, "it's daytime. The sun is shining outside."

Just then the lights go out and above us beautiful stars appear. "Oh," I gasp, "this is wonderful. It's like nighttime at the house where we used to live in the country."

"I know, Terry," Daddy says with a sigh. "That's why I like to come here. In the big city you can't see the stars at night. So that machine over there puts pictures of the stars up on this ceiling."

We sit and watch the program. There's music and talking. A man tells some of the names of the stars and how far away they are.

I look and look. I remember some of the stars from our country home. My daddy showed them to me a long time ago.

When the program is over, we just sit and sit, thinking about all those beautiful stars. Daddy leans over and says a Bible verse. " 'When you look up at the sky, you see the sun, moon and stars. The Lord your God has made these things for all people everywhere.' "

Then I whisper, "Thank You, Jesus, for making the stars for me."—C.M.

Mr. Weatherby's Partner

I go to bed and sleep in peace. Lord, only you keep me safe. Ps. 4:8, ICB.

"Hello, Mr. Weatherby," I say as I climb the steps to our apartment building. "How are you?"

Mr. Weatherby smiles and waves at me. "I'm just fine, Terry. How's the family?"

I sit down beside Mr. Weatherby and tell him about the planetarium and the beautiful stars I saw there. He listens and nods his head. Mr. Weatherby likes it when I talk to him.

"Are you guarding the apartment again tonight?" I ask.

"That's my job," he says. "I want to make sure you're safe and sound all night, so I'll keep my eyes and ears open for trouble."

"Thank you, Mr. Weatherby," I say as I head for the stairs. "I'm glad you and Jesus are watching out for me."

"Me and who?"

"Jesus," I repeat. "He guards me too. I learned a verse in Sabbath school. It says, 'I go to bed and sleep in peace. Lord, only you keep me safe. Of course, I know you're helping, so I feel very safe when I'm sleeping in my bed."

"Well, well," Mr. Weatherby says with a chuckle. "Me and Jesus, huh? Sounds like I've got a good Partner."

I wave and go up the stairs. Mr. Weatherby turns and looks out toward the street. He's got work to do.—C.M.

Jesus Can See You Anywhere

Yes, I am sure that nothing can separate us from the love God has for us. Rom. 8:38, ICB.

Mommy, Daddy, and I are going to a big store on the other side of the city. Daddy says we'll ride on something called a subway. He tells me a subway is a big tunnel that goes under the city with trains traveling through them. Sounds kinda scary to me.

We take a taxi to the subway station, then go down, down, down under the city streets.

Rumble. Rumble. Rattle. Rattle. The big trains rush past us. I hold Mommy's hand tightly.

"Terry, are you frightened by all these noisy trains?" my daddy asks.

"Yes," I say, trying to be brave. Then I suddenly have a really scary thought. "Daddy," I call, "can Jesus see us way down in this tunnel under the city?"

Daddy smiles and picks me up in his arms. "Of course He can," he says. "Jesus can see you anywhere and anytime, even down in a subway."

I watch the trains rush by. I listen to the rattles and rumbles. I see the people getting on and off the busy trains.

Then I think of the tall buildings high above me, the streets and cars, the buses and trucks. And then I think of the big blue sky and the many, many stars high above.

Finally I think of Jesus looking down and seeing me, even in this noisy subway tunnel. I smile. I'm glad that Jesus knows where I am.

Even in the big city, Jesus can see me.—C.M.

Especially for Preschoolers

Little Talks With Jesus
Nancy Beck Irland. These preschool devotionals meet the spiritual needs and interests of little children. Written in simple language and filled with wonderful stories, they help children cultivate Christian values while giving them a personal understanding and love for Jesus. Hardcover, 252 pages. US$9.95, Cdn$12.45.

Thank You, God, for My Body
Edwina Grice Neely. Your body is fascinating when you haven't been in it for long. That's why toddlers love this book that introduces them to their bodies and their Creator. Bible verses, short rhyming prayers of thanks, and adorable illustrations are combined in this big, easy-to-hold book with a sturdy, wipe-clean cover. Hardcover, 32 pages. US$6.95, Cdn$8.70.

My Bible Friends Videos
These popular stories, told by Uncle Dan and Aunt Sue, combined with video treatment of the beautiful scenes from the books, result in five exciting videos that preschool children will want to see again and again. Each video contains four stories and is about 25 minutes in length. VHS, Beta, or PAL. US$19.95, Cdn$27.45 each. US$89.95, Cdn$123.70 set.

To order, call **1-800-765-6955** or write to ABC Mailing Service, P.O. Box 1119, Hagerstown, MD 21741. Send check or money order. Enclose applicable sales tax and 15 percent (minimum US$2.50) for postage and handling. Prices and availability subject to change without notice. Add GST in Canada.

The *Forever Stories* Collection
The great controversy for children

Forever Stories
Take your children on a fascinating journey through the events of the great controversy from the rebellion of Lucifer to the new earth. Simply written and filled with captivating illustrations, these books by Carolyn Byers make it easy for them to understand the plan of salvation. Hardcover, five volumes. US$10.95, Cdn$13.70 each. US$49.95, Cdn$62.45 set.

Forever Stories Prints
Set 1: The Young Jesus
These beautiful prints, selected from the *Forever Stories* books, capture the childhood emotions and early development of Christ. They will help children realize that their friend Jesus was young once too and that He understands their joys and sorrows. Four 16" x 20" prints, US$12.95, Cdn$16.20.

Forever Stories Coloring Books
Now children can color their favorite pictures from the *Forever Stories* books themselves! Coloring these pictures will reinforce each story's message and give your child a creative worship experience. Level 1, preschool. Level 2, early elementary. 32 pages. US$2.95, Cdn$3.70 each.